Helion & Company Limited
Unit 8 Amherst Business Centre
Budbrooke Road
Warwick
CV34 5WE
England
Tel. 01926 499 619
Email: info@helion.co.uk
Website: www.helion.co.uk
Twitter: @helionbooks

Published by Helion & Company 2019
Designed and typeset by Farr out
    Publications, Wokingham, Berkshire
Cover designed by Paul Hewitt, Battlefield
    Design (www.battlefield-design.co.uk)
Printed by Henry Ling Limited, Dorchester,
    Dorset

Text © Santiago Rivas 2019
Illustrations © as individually credited
Color profiles and maps © Luca Canossa
    2019
Diagrams © Tom Cooper 2019

ISBN 978-1-912866-39-7

British Library Cataloguing-in-Publication
    Data
A catalogue record for this book is available
    from the British Library

We always welcome receiving book
proposals from prospective authors.

CONTENTS

ABBREVIATIONS

ADF	automatic direction finding
AFB	Air Force Base (US Air Force)
AL	Alferez (2nd Lieutenant, FAA)
ARMACUAR	Area de Material Rio IV (principal workshop of the FAA, located at Rio IV)
ARA	Armada de la Republica Argentina (Argentine Navy, also used as a prefix to warship-names of the Argentine Navy)
BACE	Base Aeronaval Comandante Espora
BAM	Base Aérea Militar (Military Air Base)
BNPB	Base Naval Puerto Belgrano
BRP	bomba retardada por paracaidas (parachute-retarded bomb)
CAP	combat air patrol
CAS	close air support
CC	Capitán de Corbeta (Lieutenant Commander, COAN)
CdoFAS	Commando Fuerza Aérea Sud (Air Force Command South, FAA)
CF	Capitán de Fragata (Commander, COAN)
CIC	Centro de Información y Control (Control and Information Centre)
CN	Capitán de Navio (Captain, COAN)
COAN	Comando de la Aviación Naval Argentina (Naval Aviation Command of the Argentine Navy)
EI	Estacion de Interceptacion (Fighter-Control Station)
FAA	Fuerza Aérea Argentina (Argentine Air Force)
FMA	Fabrica Militar de Aviones
GAE	Grupo Aeronaval Embarcado (the Argentine Navy's embarked air wing)
HUD	head-up display
HMS	Her Majesty's Ship (prefix to warship-names of the Royal navy)
IFR	in-flight refuelling
ILC	interceptor listo en cubierta ('interceptor ready on deck', Argentine Navy's term for 'interceptor on quick reaction alert')
ILS	instrumental landing system
INS	instrumental navigation system
MV	Motor Vessel (modern prefix for merchant ships)
NAS	Naval Air Station (US Navy)

NATOPS	Naval Air Training and Operating Procedures Standardization
Nav/attack	navigational and attack (avionics system)
PT	Primer Teniente (1st Lieutenant, FAA)
QRA	quick reaction alert
SS	Steam Ship (old prefix for merchant ships)
TACAN	tactical air navigation system
TC	Teniente de Corbeta (Ensign, COAN)
TF	Task Force
TF	Teniente de Fragata (Lieutenant Junior Grade, COAN)
TN	Teniente de Navio (Lieutenant, COAN)
TT	Teniente (Lieutenant, FAA)
UHF	ultra high frequency
USN	US Navy
VC	Vicecomodoro (Lieutenant Colonel, FAA)
VHF	very high frequency
VLF	very low frequency
VOR	VHF omni-directional range (short-range navigation system)

Argentine and British names for geographic locations in the Falklands Archipelago[1]

Bahía Ruíz Puente	Brenton Loch and Grantham Sound
Bahía San Julián	Queen Charlotte Bay
BAM Cóndor	Goose Green airfield (grass strip)
BAM Malvinas	Port Stanley airfield (concrete strip)
Bougainville	Lively Island
Goicoechea	New Island
Islas Malvinas	Falkland Islands
Isla de Bórbon	Pebble Island
Isla Gran Malvina	West Falkland
Isla Pelada	Barren Island
Isla Soledad	East Falkland
Estación Aeronaval Calderón	Pebble Island airfield (grass strip)
Monte Dos Hermans	Two Sisters
Puerto Argentino	Port Stanley
Punta Roca Blanca	White Rock Point
Rivadavia	Wickham Hill
San Carlos Strait	Falkland Sound

INTRODUCTION

On 2 April 1982, after more than a century of issuing claims about the archipelago in the South Atlantic that the Argentines call the Malvinas, and the British call the Falklands, the government in Buenos Aires ordered an amphibious landing, opposed by the Royal Marines of Naval Party 8901, to expel the British authorities. Thus began the conflict known as the Malvinas War in Argentina, or the Falklands War in the English-speaking world.

London reacted by deploying a major task force of the Royal Navy, with orders to recover possession of the islands. Following the British recapture of South Georgia on 25 April 1982, the main combat for the islands proper began on 1 May 1982, when the Task Force reached the Falklands. From that day onwards, the Douglas A-4 Skyhawks of the Argentine Air Force (Fuerza Aérea Argentina) and the Naval Aviation Command (Comando de la Aviación Naval Argentina, COAN) performed the most important combat operations against the British forces.

The FAA acquired its first A-4B Skyhawks in 1966, in the form of 50 aircraft that equipped Grupo 5 de Caza (5th Fighter Wing) of V Brigada Aérea.[2] In 1975, these were reinforced with a batch of 25 A-4Cs acquired for Grupo 4 de Caza of IV Brigada Aérea. Meanwhile, in 1971, COAN had purchased a batch of 16 A-4Qs to equip the 3° Escuadrilla Aeronaval de Ataque, replacing its old Grumman F9F Panthers.

While both fleets were significantly downsized by attrition, they still formed the backbone of air force and naval aviation and caused the heaviest losses to the Royal Navy through sinking the destroyer HMS *Coventry* (D118), frigates HMS *Antelope* (F170) and HMS *Ardent* (F184), the landing craft *F4*, and the Round Table-class Landing Ship Logistics RFA *Sir Galahad* (L3005). Moreover, they damaged up to a dozen other ships and hit multiple ground targets. This success was

achieved at a hefty price: the Argentine A-4 Skyhawk units lost a total of 10 A-4Bs, 9 A-4Cs and 3 A-4Qs; and 18 of their pilots were killed. Unsurprisingly, the experience of the Skyhawk during the Malvinas War became the topic of many legends[3], often equalling affairs from the Vietnam War and seemingly endless wars in the Middle East. Thirty-seven years later, the FAA still fly the type: while older A-4Bs and A-4Cs have been replaced by A-4Ms and OA-4Ms upgraded to the A-4AR and OA-4AR standard, the Argentine Air Force remains one of the last two military operators of the type.

1

FIRST ORDERS

There were a number of reasons for the Argentine Air Force to replace much of its equipment in the early 1960s. The already obsolete Gloster Meteor F.Mk 4 acquired in 1947 was reaching the end of its operational life, only a quarter of the original batch of 100 examples still being available at that time. Accompanying them were twenty-five North American F-86F-40 Sabres, which were not enough to sustain the delicate regional balance; especially not vis-a-vis Chile, a country that operated de Havilland Vampires and Lockheed F-80C Shooting Stars and was about to acquire Hawker Hunters from the United Kingdom. Moreover, the Brazilian Air Force was equipped with the Gloster Meteor F.Mk 8 and Lockheed F-80 Shooting Star. Other forces, such as Peru, were in talks to acquire the Dassault Mirage V and in this way, receive the newest generation of supersonic fighters – well ahead of Argentina. Furthermore, the FAA had in its inventory some FMA IA-35 Huanquero armed transports, Beech B-45 Mentor, Morane Saulnier MS.760 Paris and North American T-28A Trojan trainers with a limited attack capacity – all in need of replacement. Such concerns were confirmed when in 1965, despite a period when the country was ruled by a constitutional government that was markedly austere and pacifist, there was a large armed confrontation over an old border dispute with Chile in the area of Laguna del Desierto: the situation escalated to the verge of war, and ended with one death on the part of Chile. This situation served to boost the need for the modernization of military aviation – unfortunately, just around the time of significant budget cuts, which limited the chances of obtaining the equipment the air force actually wanted. After evaluating different models, according to availability and budgetary possibilities, the FAA concluded that the Douglas A-4B Skyhawk was the one best suited for its needs. One of the reasons was that the aircraft was equipped with a hook for landing on aircraft carriers: this made it compatible with the arresting wires installed at the end of Argentine military runways and could be used to stop aircraft in the event of an emergency – a procedure that proved far safer than the then frequently used arresting nets. The decision was made and Buenos Aires thus

placed an order for 50 A-4Bs that had been withdrawn from service with the US Navy (USN) and stored at Lichfield Park in Arizona.

The First Order

Upon receiving the Argentine request for Skyhawks – which included provision for the conversion training of pilots and ground crews, and a large shipment of spare parts – the Douglas company proposed to modify the 50 aircraft through the addition of advanced components, including spoilers from the A-4F variant; installation of the Bendix CAN-4 navigation system instead of the old AN/ASQ-17; the addition of a very-high-frequency omni-directional range (VOR) receiver in the tail; the addition of a Bendix RTA-41B/RNA-26C radio with an antenna located behind the cockpit; the installation of the ADF-73 complex in a dorsal housing instead of the AN/ARA-25; and the addition of the UHF AN/ARC-27 and the AN/APX-6BG identification friend-foe (IFF) system. The Argentines accepted such ideas and went a few steps further: during the modifications the TACAN AN/ARN-21 and the AN/APN-141 altimeter were also eliminated. The result was the emergence of the variant actually designated the A-4P. Nevertheless, the FAA preferred to continue calling its first batch of Skyhawks the A-4B, and they will be referred to as such in this book.

On 29 October 1965, the contract between the Argentine air force and Douglas 'ad referendum' of their respective governments was signed. All 50 aircraft were ready for delivery – painted in silver-grey overall and serialled from C-201 to C-250 – by June 1966, while the first group of pilots and ground crews had entered their conversion

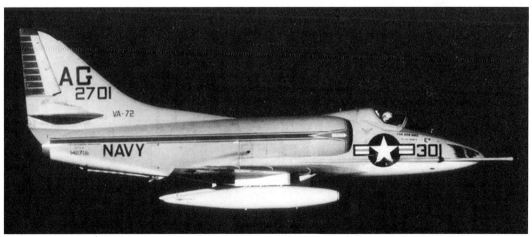

The A-4B that would become C-211 of the FAA, flying for squadron VA-72 of the US Navy.
(All photographs are from the Santiago Rivas Collection, unless stated otherwise)

C-203 was to be the sole Argentine A-4B that would not reach the country, as it was lost on 1 August 1966 in an accident in Kansas. The pilot, Captain José Luis Rodriguez Morell, ejected.

Howard Air Force Base in the Panama Canal Zone during the first ferry flight. The pilot is Captain Luis Héctor Destri, who flew the C-213.

The A-4Bs replaced the Avro Lincolns with V Brigada Aérea. In the bomber-role Lincolns would be replaced by BAC Canberras.

training at the Douglas facilities in Tulsa in February of the same year. The flight personnel of Grupo 5 de Caza (5th Fighter Wing), V Brigada Aérea under the command of Vicecomodorro (VC) Jorge A Mones Ruiz, and ground crews led by VC Palauzelos then started their conversion training at Olathe airfield in Kansas.[1] All conversion training was run on the Argentine aircraft. One of them never reached its destination: on 1 August 1966, C-203 suffered a fuel pump failure while on final approach and crashed. Its pilot, Capitán José Luis Rodriguez Morell ejected safely.

In parallel, the Naval Aviation carried out its own negotiations for the incorporation of the same type of machines, although with without a positive outcome. The successful management of the FAA undoubtedly gave ground to the aspirations of the COAN to acquire the same type six years later.

Once the conversion training was complete, the entire Grupo 5 de Caza transferred its new aircraft from Olathe, via Naval Air Station (NAS) Cecil Field, NAS Guantanamo Bay on Cuba, Howard Air Force Base (AFB) in Panama, Chichlayo (in Peru), and San Miguel de Tucumán in Argentina, to its home base of Military Air Base (Base Aérea Militar, BAM) Villa Reynolds, outside the city of Villa Mercedes in the Argentine province of San Luis, between 28 and 31 October 1966. The first 12 aircraft entered service with Halcón Squadron, commanded by VC Mones Ruiz, itself then a part of Grupo 4 de Caza Bombardeo of V Brigada Aérea.[2] During this epic 11,000-kilometre-long flight, the formation was supported by Douglas C-45 transport serial number T-45, and Grumman SA-16B Albatros serial number BS-02. On arrival, their pilots were received by the commander of V Brigada Aérea, Comodoro Alberto Chiostri, who after exchanging the corresponding greetings, gave way to the ceremony presided over by the commander-in-chief of the FAA, Brigadier General Adolfo Teodoro Álvarez, who spoke from a platform beneath three Avro Lincoln bombers.

With the addition of the A-4B, the first qualitative, technological and quantitative leap was made since the incorporation of the Meteor almost 20 years earlier. This brought with it a training program carried out in the USA, which was delivered without problems thanks to the capacity and commitment of the men of the FAA.

Early Operational Service

Grupo 4 de Caza Bombardeo was declared fully operational on 18 March 1967, by when it was reorganised as Grupo 5 de Caza Bombardeo (still assigned to V Brigada Aérea). By this time, the second batch of 12 aircraft had arrived to form the second squadron. However, because of the Vietnam War, it would take more than two years for the FAA to receive its remaining A-4Bs. Meanwhile, the training of the Argentine crews was continued in the USA, and included in-flight refuelling (IFR) with the help of Douglas-made 'buddy packs' (enabling one Skyhawk to refuel another): that said, the FAA stored the IFR-probes of its A-4Bs for most of the next dozen years. Their removal slightly improved the flight characteristics, and it was only in 1979 that Argentina finally acquired dedicated tanker aircraft in the form of a pair of Locheed KC-130H Hercules aircraft (serial numbers TC-69 and TC-70).

In 1967 the instruction of new pilots also began, and on 6 September the first solo flight was made in a Skyhawk by PT William Lehmann, followed by several others. Operational exercises began a year later: on 29 August, Operation Magdalena was initiated during which all pilots reached the required level of qualification, while on 9 and 10 November the units flew air-to-ground exercises against targets on the range off Mazurca Island in the Parana Delta. Finally, on 22 May 1969 the Argentine Skyhawk units took part in Exercise Comprobación II, during which they flew simulated airstrikes on BAM Mar del Plata, which was defended by old Meteors.

The third batch of 12 Skyhawks for Argentina was ferried in June 1969, this time along the route from Richard Gebhard AFB, via NAS Jacksonville, NAS Key West, Kingston (Jamaica), Howard AFB (in Panama), Talara and Pisco (Peru), to Villa Reynolds. With this, all of the 49 surviving aircraft were now in Argentina. This, the final batch of A-4Bs, arrived wearing camouflage colours of brown and green – and had these applied in the opposite way to the scheme applied to other Skyhawks in Argentina.

Into Service

With the arrival of all of its aircraft, V Brigada Aérea became a main combat unit, despite having some problems in the supply of spare parts and in the logistics organization: the Skyhawk was not only much more modern, but also available in much higher numbers than the old Lincolns and Lancasters, even though the role of the latter was taken over by Canberras of II Brigada Aérea. Another problem was the short life of the

Skyhawk engines between inspections: this was barely reaching 150 hours, forcing the ground crews to constantly change powerplants to keep the highest possible number of aircraft in fully mission capable condition. Nevertheless, through all the years in which the Skyhawks were in service, the annual flight plan was fulfilled.

Meanwhile, in 1972 the unit organised the "Halcones Azules" aerobatic team that successfully carried out two demonstrations during the year, the first in the province of Jujuy and the other at Ezeiza International Airport near the city of Buenos Aires. For the exhibition flights, six aircraft flew in formation, while two flew solo and another, called "Sónico" (Sonic), plunged from a great height to break the sound barrier. After several exhibitions the following year, such as the one closing the Aeronautic and Space Week of 1973 in Paraná, where they demonstrated air-to-ground shooting in the Paraná River and in-flight refuelling, the team was deactivated.

Meanwhile, the exercises continued, with operations Comprobación V of 16 October and Surubí I of 29 November 1972, which included a simulated attack on II Brigada Aérea at BAM Paraná in Entre Ríos, and a demonstration of air-to-ground shooting with 70mm rockets. In 1974, the Skyhawks took part in Operation Golfo – from 24 to 30 June – including a re-deployment to BAM Comodoro Rivadavia in Chubut province.[3] This was followed by operations Orión I and Orión II, on 27 June and 9-12 September, respectively, during which 7 aircraft and then 16 aircraft were re-deployed. Otherwise, the Skyhawks ran their routine training operations from their base to the training ranges of Antuna and Salinas del Bebedero in San Luis, and in Las Lajas in the province of Mendoza. Furthermore, to celebrate the Day of the Air Force, 39 aircraft flew to VII Brigada Aérea at BAM Morón, near the city of Buenos Aires, on 10 August 1974 within the frame of Operation Revista, which included a parade in front of President María Estela Martínez de Perón. On this occasion, the largest number of A-4s could be seen outside V Brigada Aérea's home base and this was one of the largest concentrations of FAA aircraft in its history. Finally, the A-4Bs were displayed on the ground and then paraded at the nearby I Brigada Aérea's home base at BAM El Palomar.

Baptism of Fire

Since 1973, the activity of the communist guerrillas that ravaged the country had increased notably due to the inability of the governments

C-216 shortly after its arrival with V Brigada Aérea. (Photo Comodoro Lusberto Medina)

C-237 in the United States together with a US Navy A-4C. Part of the third ferry
flight, this batch was the first delivered in camouflage colours. From 1969 the
aircraft of the first two batches had camouflage applied in Argentina.

The A-4Bs of the last ferry flight to leave the United States. The camouflage applied
in the USA was applied in the 'negative' of the pattern applied in Argentina.

of Héctor Campora, Juan. D. Perón and his widow, María Estela Martínez, to control the subversives. The high point was reached in 1975, when the Revolutionary Army of the People (Ejército Revolucionario del Pueblo, ERP) launched a rural insurgency in the difficult-to-access mountains and jungles of southwestern Tucumán province with the intention of creating a liberated zone. In the light of the growing crisis, on 5 February 1975, the president of Argentina signed the secret Decree 261, ordering the armed forces and the police to annihilate 'subversive elements' in Operation Independencia. In support of this enterprise, the FAA launched Operation Torión, which included close air support (CAS) missions. To evaluate possible courses of action, on 6 November 1975 a squadron of A-4Bs flew airstrikes on guerrilla camps, deploying fragmentation bombs and supporting friendly troops with their 20mm cannons. On 18 November 1975, the unit flew a total of 14 CAS sorties, all the time supported by Beech B-45 Mentor training aircraft of the School of Military Aviation that acted as forward air controllers (FACs). Subsequently, the brand-new FMA IA.58 Pucara counterinsurgency (COIN) strikers, English Electric

C-201 just after being repainted in camouflage colours at the beginning of 1969, keeping the large roundel
and national flag and painted with semi-gloss paint. Notable is the lack of the refuelling probe.

A line of Mirage IIIEAs and more than 30 A-4Bs during the celebrations of the Argentine Air Force Day on 10 August 1974, when a parade and flypast took place at VII Air Brigade in Morón.

C-242 seen on 7 July 1971, one year after its arrival in the country, deployed at Morón Air Base for a military parade on 9 July, the Argentine Independence Day.

A line of A-4Bs in 1972, showing the paint scheme used in the 1970s. (Horacio Gareiso)

Canberra bombers, and even Morane Saulnier Paris trainers joined the action.

The A-4B Skyhawks flew additional airstrikes on 19 December 1975, this time against a mutiny within the air force, led by Comodoro Jesús Capellini, who brought BAM Jorge Newbery in the centre of Buenos Aires, and BAM Morón – the homebase of VII Brigada Aérea – under his control. Operating from the home base of VIII Brigada Aérea in José C. Paz, the A-4s bombed Moron, reportedly destroying at least one B-45 Mentor in the process. Their action prompted the mutineers to give up.

2

FOLLOW-UPS

The third important event in the history of the FAA in 1975 was the acquisition of 25 Douglas A-4Cs with the aim of replacing the veteran F-86F Sabres.[1] Stored at Davis Monthan, these aircraft were acquired without any inspections or upgrade: the Americans only removed their AN/AJB-3 low-altitude bombing systems, while leaving the autopilot and the gyroscope-based navigational-attack system (nav/attack) in place. Many were worn out after being flown by the US Navy during the Vietnam War, both from aircraft carriers and from ground bases, but were then not flown for quite a period of time.

The A-4Cs were delivered by ship to Buenos Aires, from where all were transferred to the Area de Material Rio IV (ARMACUAR), re-assembled, inspected and then pressed into service – a process that advanced at only a slow pace. The first four A-4Cs – serials C-301 to C-304 – were delivered to IV Brigada Aérea at Mendoza only on 7 April 1976, in a formation led by Sabarret, the deputy commander of the unit. They subsequently entered service with Grupo 1 de Cazabombardeo. The Air Operations Command of the FAA then ordered V Brigada Aérea to support the further build-up of the squadrons through the provision of six pilots to act as instructors and lend their support and experience to the personnel at Mendoza. Mendoza also received arrester cables at the end of the runway by September 1976. Eventually, by the end of the year, ARMACUAR delivered 12 A-4Cs to IV Brigada Aérea. The aircraft with the serial C-320 followed in early 1977, and others – up to serial C-325 – by the first half of 1978. However, in the meantime two further A-4Cs that had not yet been delivered to IV Brigada Aérea had already been written off: on 2 November 1976, serial numbers C-316 and C-317 collided in flight over the towns of Luis Palacios and Aldao (Santa Fe province), and their pilots – Teniente (TT) Reynaldo Vitale and Primer Teninente (PT) Valentin Acosta were forced to eject.

Overall, the condition of the A-4Cs was not the best and the FAA was forced to work hard to improve their condition. Starting in 1979

The A-4C that would become C-302 in Argentina, during a fuel tank ejection test while serving with squadron VA-83 of the US Navy.

The A-4C that would become C-309 in Argentina, before delivery and still stored. On 21 May 1982 it was shot down by a Sea Harrier over the Malvinas/Falklands.

The A-4C serial C-313 shortly after arriving at its base in Mendoza, with the first paint scheme used by the planes. This one has its nose in white.

it took care replace older AN/APC-141 IFF-systems with the IFF-2720 and the ARN-21 TACAN. A year later, their AN/APG-53A radars were replaced by VLF/Omega Litton LTN-211 Program 2700 nav/attack systems, supplemented by French-made Thomson-CSF AHV.611 radio altimeters (instead of US-made AN/APN-141s). Furthermore, because a US arms embargo blocked the delivery of 29 Wright J-65W-16A engines for A-4Bs, and 32 Wright J-65W-20 engines for A-4Cs, the technicians of ARMACUAR installed several of the latter – which were slightly more powerful – into the A-4Bs. To more easily differentiate the aircraft in question, they had the tip of the nose painted in white instead of the usual black.

The Beagle Channel Crisis

In mid-1978, and in view of the possibility of a border conflict with Chile, the A-4Cs were wired to carry Israeli-made Rafael Shafrir Mk.2 short-range infrared-homing air-to-air missiles. These were installed by Argentine personnel under the supervision of Israeli Lieutenant-Colonel Shlomo Shapira, who also provided the necessary instruction for Argentine pilots – not only in the use of Shafrirs, but also with regards to air combat with the A-4. IV Brigada Aérea received a total of 26 launch rails for Shafrir, but only seven aircraft were modified to carry them. The operational evaluation of the new armament was carried out at Base Aeronaval Comandante Espora (BACE) on 10 October 1978 and included several live firings.

In addition, to maintain the qualifications of the pilots, Exercise Poder de Fuego (Fire Power) was performed – in cooperation with A-4Bs – during which AN-M65 bombs, Zuni 127mm rockets and 20mm internal cannons were deployed against targets at the Las Lajas range. This was followed by

A line of A-4Cs shortly after arriving in the country. The first two aircraft did not have their guns installed.

An A-4C on a very low flypast in the 1970s.

A-4C serial C-318 (amongst others) landing at BAM San Julián armed with Shafrir 2 missiles during the deployment for the crisis with Chile in December 1978.

A-4B C-241 and A-4C C-315 shortly after the arrival of the latter in Argentina, before receiving the badge of Grupo 4 de Caza.

An A-4C armed with Shafrir 2 missiles deployed at BAM San Julián during the crisis with Chile in December 1978.

Exercise Efectos, during which pilots trained for the deployment of 68mm unguided rockets from LAU-61 pods.

Finally, in light of the tensions with Chile, the FAA decided to establish a permanent presence at BAM Río Gallegos and each combat squadron – regardless if equipped with Dassault Mirage IIIEA, Israeli Aircraft Industries Mirage 5/Dagger, or A-4Bs or Cs – had to regularly rotate its aircraft to this air base. The units that had two squadrons (Grupo 5 and 6 de Caza) deployed one for half of the month and the other the other half.[2] Those which had one squadron did so with half of the squadron in each half of the month. At the time of the Argentine landings on the Falklands/Malvinas, Grupo 4 de Caza had half of its operational A-4Cs deployed at BAM Río Gallegos.

Table 1: Acquisitions of A-4s by the FAA and their Status in 1982		
Number of Aircraft and Variant	Unit	Number of Aircraft available in 1982
50 A-4B	V Brigada Aérea	36
25 A-4C	IV Brigada Aérea	19

3

SKYHAWKS FOR THE NAVY

Because of the obsolescence of its primary combat aircraft, in 1963 the Argentine Naval Aviation Command decided to replace the Vought F4U-5 Corsair and Grumman F9F-2 Panther, and generated a series of studies concluding that the best aircraft to replace the Corsair was the Douglas AD-5 Skyraider, and that to replace the Panther with was the Douglas A-4 Skyhawk. In mid-1966 the Navy was interested in acquiring the A-4B. The United States offered a batch of 30 A-4A but these were not considered. In 1968, the request was made to buy 10 A-4F and two TA-4F aircraft but this time the Americans refused. For this reason, in 1969, a quotation was requested from Great Britain for twelve Hawker Siddeley Harrier GR.Mk 1 aircraft with vertical take-off and landing capability. Taking advantage of the transfer to Argentina of the aircraft carrier ARA *25 de Mayo* (V-2), recently acquired from the Dutch navy, tests were carried out on its flight deck on 4 September 1969.[1] To counter the potential purchase of the British aircraft, the United States then quickly offered the A-4B Skyhawk and reached an agreement with the Argentines.

The Naval Aviation decided that its aircraft would have different equipment to the A-4Bs in service with the FAA since 1966: it retained the TACAN, ADF, VOR/ILS, UHF/VHF (contrary to the FAA's A-4Bs where the TACAN and the UHF were deleted). Therefore, a commission travelled to Villa Reynolds, where everything related to the equipment was studied and discussed and a decision taken for the wings of the Navy's aircraft to be equipped with spoilers, in addition to a more powerful engine (the one that corresponded to the A-4C).

Taking advantage of the fact that the BAe HS.125 Dominie acquired for the country was to be ferried to Argentina, Rear Admiral Hermes Quijada had meanwhile visited Israel to exchange opinions and information, since the Israeli A-4E pilots had obtained extensive combat experience in the War of Attrition against Egypt and Syria, fought since 1967. The result was a request to expand the acquisition through additional A-4Bs upgraded to A-4Q standard,

and a few A-4Bs to be used as advanced trainers. Rather reluctantly, Washington granted permission for the delivery of 16 A-4Qs and 8 A-4Bs (the latter to be used as a source of spares only), worth US$5 million. The related contract was signed on 1 May 1971, and included the provision of conversion training for the pilots of V Brigada Aérea, as well as for Teniente de Frigata (TF) Julio Lavezzo to perform flight tests in Dallas, and undergo a landing signal officer (LSI) course with the VT-21 squadron of the US Navy. Selected pilots then underwent conversion training with another squadron of the US Navy, VA-127, and ran carrier qualifications on board the aircraft carrier USS *Coral Sea* (CV-43).

Conversion Training and Testing

During the carrier daytime qualifications, a very unusual incident occurred in which Capitán de Corbeta (CC) Invierno was the protagonist. Underway over the Pacific Ocean in marginal meteorological conditions, he was low on fuel. There were eight other aircraft in the landing pattern over USS *Coral Sea*, and the landing deck was closed. Due to the bad weather the flight controller ordered him to land on an alternative site on the mainland. Running short on fuel, and flying through a thick cloud layer, Invierno eventually found a patch of land and a small airfield – and promptly landed there – without knowing where he was. He spent the night and the next day there, waiting for the weather to improve before he returned safely to the ship.

Meanwhile, part of the COAN commission visited the USA and CCs Invierno (the future unit commander) and Nabias, and Tenientes de Navío (TNs) Saralegui and Troitino, travelled to Jacksonville, where they would carry out test flights at the factory. After each flying five hours, they found the aircraft in good condition, and then developed a conversion training program similar to that run for the FAA a few years earlier – but modified through the addition of AIM-

The A-4Q 0655/ 3-A-202 on the Estados Unidos during the training flights. Initially they carried on the callsign the "3-", and they were painted with the Argentine Navy badge on the rear part of the fuselage in front of the word "Naval". After arriving to Argentina the "3-" was removed and painted again in 1974, when the callsigns passed from 201 to 216 to 301 to 316, the badge was removed and the word "Naval" was changed for "Armada".

9B Sidewinder short-range infrared-homing air-to-air missiles and Sergeant Fletcher buddy packs (with a capacity of 900 litres) right from the start.[2] That said, once again, the Americans actually attempted to outsmart the Argentines and banned the export of AIM-9Bs. The Israelis promptly offered their Shafrir Mk.2s, to which the Americans reacted by offering their – inferior – AIM-9Bs at far more favourable prices. The Argentines eventually purchased the Sidewinders from the USA but bought buddy packs from Israel.

Operational Conversion

Once all the aircraft were in Jacksonville, on 7 February they embarked on the aircraft carrier ARA *25 de Mayo* with all the spares and ammunition. The ship sailed on 10 February to Puerto Belgrano Naval Base (BNPB) and arrived on 3 March in the morning hours, where the aircraft were all assigned to 3° Escuadrilla Aeronaval de Caza y Ataque.[3] The original idea was to form a flotilla composed of two squadrons, one for training (8 A-4B) and one operational (16 A-4Q). This idea could not be carried out afterwards and only remained as 3° Escuadrilla of the Escuadra Aeronaval No.3.

3-A-209 received the honour of being the first Skyhawk to make a landing aboard ARA *25 de Mayo*, on 14 August 1972, under the command of CC Invierno. Two days later the first catapult launch was also made. Weapons training was carried out at BAM Trelew and the Isla Verde ranges.

Meanwhile, a commission composed of technicians of the unit travelled to Australia from 28 June to 14 July 1972, to embark the aircraft carrier HMAS *Melbourne* and collect experience of the A-4G variant, because that combination of ship and aircraft was similar to what the Argentine Navy was about to acquire. Of particular interest was the experience that during

TN Ítalo Lavezzo after his solo flight in an A-4Q in the United States in July 1971. This was the sole A-4Q to receive the word "Armada" on the front part of the fuselage.

Photo taken aboard ARA *25 de Mayo* on 14 October 1972, during launch tests after an incident occurred with the impact of a strobe against a LAU-32G rocket launcher on the central pylon.

A-4Q 0664/3-A-211 in 1972. This aircraft was lost in an accident five years later.

The A-4Qs were the first aircraft to operate regularly from an aircraft carrier in Argentina. Previously, only a Grumman Panther had landed once on ARA *Independencia*.

A-4Qs on board ARA *25 de Mayo* on the first carrier operations of the model in October 1972.

it had become hooked on the accelerator. The US report thus confirmed the Argentine NCO's assessment. The loss of control that TF Peña suffered was a situation that at the time was also under investigation in the USA, where it resulted in a large study: sadly, its results reached Argentina only after the fatal accident involving TN Eduarto Marty (on 3A-215) on 25 June 1973, in Monte Hermoso, Bahia Blanca. Marty managed to eject but was never recovered. Whilst in a vertical loop, the elevator came out of the air flow, losing lift and then control of the aircraft.

Exercises

Meanwhile, in September 1972, COAN Skyhawks participated in their first exercise, UNITAS XIII, together with the US Navy. In 1973, when the unit it became dependent on the 3° Escuadra Aeronaval, it changed all the serials of its aircraft to the range 3-A-301 to 3-A-316. On 30 April 1974, the unit experienced its third accident, when 3-A-305 flown by TF Roberto Curilovic and 3-A-314 flown by TN Augusto Bedacarratz collided in flight, losing the bow and the horizontal stabiliser, respectively. Fortunately, both pilots were able to land safely.

These accidents evidenced the need for pilots to receive training in two-seater aircraft, prompting the evaluation of a possible purchase of two TA-4Js – which in turn prompted Lockheed to offer to modify two aircraft in the way subsequently realised with Singapore's TA-4S. However, no such ideas could be realised due to a lack of money. Instead, an agreement was reached with Washington to provide pilots with additional training with the USN VT-21 and VT-22 squadrons, both of which were equipped with TA-4Js.

The fourth – and the third fatal – accident occurred on 13 June 1975 when TF Echegoyen made a 'bolter' with 3-A-310. A bolter occurs when an aircraft attempting an arrested landing on the flight deck touches down but fails to catch an arrestor wire. Echegoyen's Skyhawk thus rolled over the port side of the deck: the pilot ejected outside his seat's limitations and was killed.

Teniente de Fragata Carlos Sánchez Alvarado was involved in a flight accident on 23 September 1975, when attempting a landing with 3-A-313: the arrestor wire No. 1 snapped and the aircraft rolled over the end of the landing deck. This time the pilot ejected in time and he landed by parachute back on the deck of the carrier. The wind blew him into the sea however, and he was recovered by Alouette III helicopter registration 3-H-9.

the catapult launch the type AA.Mk 1 strobe recovery equipment worked improperly, repeatedly causing damage to the aircraft.

Such issues aside, the introduction to service of the A-4Q was a great technological leap forward for the COAN and the entire Argentine Navy. For the first time ever, the Embarked Air Group (Grupo Aeronaval Embarcado, GAE) had a modern and effective fighter jet in its complement, armed with infrared homing air-to-air missiles, and capable of IFR: no other navy in Latin America obtained a similar capability until Brazil did so in 1999.

On 16 January 1973, TF Mario Peña – who had recently returned from the United States to perform the adaptation of the A-4 – made a flight in formation with TN Carlos Ruiz in the vicinity of Base Aeronaval Comandante Espora (BACE). Both started a loop, with Lieutenant Peña as wingman (flying 3-A-216). Exiting the manoeuvre, the aircraft flipped out of control and Peña ejected: the hose of his oxygen mask remained hooked to the throttle lever and he was killed. After this unfortunate accident, a report came from the United States regarding this danger, stating that the hose should be passed through an eyelet. When Survival Officer Dreiling made his investigation, he found the helmet of the pilot and discovered that the mask holder on the helmet was fastened but without the mask. He deduced that

ARA *25 de Mayo* during the crisis with Chile, with eleven A-4Q Skyhawks, four S-2E Trackers and three S-61D Sea Kings.

0661/3-A-308 on ARA *25 de Mayo* in December 1978, when they almost entered combat with Chile.

3-A-304 using the Sargent Fletcher 'buddy pack' for in-flight refuelling.

In 1974, the escadrille was visited by an Israeli pilot who had flown the A-4E and shared the latest experiences from the June 1967 War, the War of Attrition and the October 1973 Arab-Israeli War. The years 1977 to 1979 were the splendour of the 3° Escuadrilla, when they operated from the aircraft carrier with up to eleven A-4Qs. In 1976, the possibility emerged for Argentina to buy 20 (subsequently reduced to 18) additional A-4Cs, followed by four additional A-4Cs and four TA-4Js (the latter were to be created by combining the rear fuselage and the wings of stored single-seaters, with new forward fuselages). Indeed, at the same time Washington made a similar proposal to the Uruguayan Air Force: however, the lack of necessary funding

prevented the realisation of this design. Instead, the decision was taken to press into service two of the A-4Bs and for this purpose they received new wings and noses (those from standard A-4Qs). Related works began during the same year but were suspended two years later: their parts were subsequently used to return additional A-4Qs to service for the 1982 conflict.

The idea of obtaining additional A-4s remained nevertheless, and in 1977 Buenos Aires asked for terms of delivery for a batch of A-4Fs. However, the US government refused to deliver, citing the lack of available aircraft. After discarding the option of buying newly-built A-4Ms, the Argentines then opted for the purchase of either the Dassault Super Etendard or British Aerospace Sea Harrier FRS.Mk 1, with the aim of receiving these by 1984 to replace ageing A-4Qs. Ultimately, this idea had to be abandoned for the lack of funding.

During 1977 and 1978 most of the pilots achieved the qualification of "Centurion", which meant that they had made more than 100 arrested landings on board ARA *25 de Mayo*. During the seventh sea stage the evaluation of night operations with the A-4Q was carried out on the aircraft carrier, where all the pilots of the squadron were catapulted at night. Only one landing was made at dawn by TN Augusto Bedacarratz. The commander of the fleet suspended the evaluation and operations were only conducted during the day or twilight, this meant that they could launch at night and thus have the ability to attack the enemy at dawn.

Tensions with Chile

On 28 September 1977, while exercises were being carried out with the aircraft carrier, the destroyer ARA *Comodoro Py* (D27) detected an unidentified aircraft off the coast of the province of Santa Cruz and ordered the scramble of an A-4Q to intercept it, although contact was lost contact before the take-off actually took place. Shortly thereafter, on 3 February 1978, five A-4Qs were deployed to Base Aeronaval Almirante Zar, in Trelew, as part of Operation Rigel, while a destroyer was deployed to the area to perform radar detection of any possible intruders. Once again, the reason was a high state of tensions with Chile. Sensing the seriousness of the situation, 3° Escuadrilla intensified its training, and in March 1978 CC Levezzo was the first of its pilots to launch two AIM-9Bs from A-4Q 3-A-301. At that time, a purchase of more advanced AIM-9E or AIM-9J missiles was studied, and the plans were made to re-equip the aircraft with more effective French-made DEFA 30mm cannons, as the Israelis had done before, and the FAA after. However, for the time being there was not enough money to implement such ideas.

The dispute with Chile over the Beagle Channel remained heightened for the rest of the year, requiring the escadrille to maintain a high level of readiness. Towards the end of 1978, when the crisis almost became an open war, the unit had 17 qualified pilots and 11 operational aircraft, and a decision was made to re-deploy it to Mendoza,

A-4Qs armed with bombs and rocket launchers aboard the carrier.
Behind are four destroyers of the Argentine Navy.

Skyhawk 0662/ 3-A-309 armed with ten Mk.81 250-pound
bombs. The front internal position of the Multiple Ejector Racks
was not used, as the bombs could hit the landing gear doors.

A-4Qs 3-A-307 and 314 were two of the three A-4Qs lost in
combat on 21 May 1982 after attacking HMS Ardent.

Table 2: Acquisitions of A-4s by COAN and their Status in 1982		
Number of Aircraft and Variant	Unit	Number of Aircraft available in 1982
16 A-4Q	3° Escuadrilla	11
8 A-4B	-	all used as sources of spares only

for dissimilar air combat manoeuvring exercise against F-86F Sabres. Hardly back from that exercise, it became known that a Learjet 25 of the Chilean Air Force had overflown Base Aeronaval Almirante Zar in Trelew. Therefore, six A-4Qs became involved in Operation Rigel II, lasting from 31 August until 7 September, during which they stood quick reaction alert (QRA) to intercept possible intruders with the help of the destroyer ARA *Piedrabuena* acting as a radar picket. Moreover, ground crews prepared triple ejector racks (TERs) loaded with LAU-69 launchers for 19 68mm rockets each, multiple ejector racks (MERs) each loaded with six Mk.82 bombs equipped with Mk. 12 Snakeye retarding fins and four-tube LAU-10 launchers for ZUNI Mk.25 127mm unguided rockets. Planned operations included cooperation with Grumman S-2E Tracker anti-submarine aircraft and Lockheed SP-2H Neptune maritime patrol aircraft. For nocturnal operations, each A-4Q was to be equipped with Mk.24 and Mk.45 flares. It was in the course of this crisis that the aircraft serial 3-A-309 was the first to ever be equipped with a locally manufactured chaff and flare dispenser. The task of preparing all of this armament and equipment was the job of TF Petinari, who went as far as to take intervalometres from the old F4U Corsairs and install them on the unit's Skyhawks this device helped release bombs following a pre-selected sequence.

On 8 December, the entire Argentine Navy – including its sole aircraft carrier with 11 A-4Qs embarked – was deployed to the south within the framework of Operation Tronador. Once within the conflict zone, squadron commander CC Ítalo Lavezzo ordered his men to fly reconnaissance and patrol missions, making two interceptions of Chilean aircraft that were tracking the fleet to the east of Tierra del Fuego: for this purpose, a pair of A-4Qs each armed with two Sidewinder missiles was kept on quick reaction alert status (in Argentine Navy parlance: 'interceptor listo en cubierta', ILC) at all times. Intercept missions and patrols were usually flown by single aircraft though.

The first interception was carried out by the squadron commander on 15 December at 2:40 p.m., at the controls of 3-A-301, together with TF Poch in 3-A-307, which were launched after the detection of two targets by radar. Upon finding the first of them, it turned out to be a friendly S-2A Tracker on a transport flight from Rio Grande to Ushuaia, while they later intercepted a CASA C-212 Aviocar of the Chilean Navy, flying at 5,000 feet, that was tracking the fleet east of Tierra del Fuego. Lavezzo activated the armament panel and selected the missiles, asking for instructions, but was instructed by the commander of the fleet, Admiral Barbuzi, not to fire but to report the position and movements of the C-212. After passing close to the Chilean aircraft, he began the return to the aircraft carrier, while the C-212 tried to fly as fast as possible into cloud in order to get out of sight. At no time was there any radio contact. The following interception was carried out by TF Petinari on 3-A-301, who – at 04:49 hours in the morning of 19 December – had caught another CASA 212 aircraft carrying out the same mission as the previous one but now flying at 3,000 feet.

Final Exercises and Testing

In 1979, although the tension with Chile had diminished after the crisis was resolved with the intervention of the Vatican, the force maintained its presence in the south, deploying A-4Qs to Base Aeronaval Rio Grande, and then – from 28 May until 9 June – from the sole Argentine aircraft carrier. This proved a good opportunity for testing Type 375 napalm bombs acquired from Spain, US-made 250lb (125kg) Mk.81 bombs, and locally-manufactured LACO rocket launchers with 7 or 19 tubes for the EDESA Albatros 96mm unguided rockets. Furthermore, during Operation Gaviota, on 5 November 1979, Condib Mk.70 anti-runway bombs of 70 kg were tested. From 27 until 11 July 1980, the Skyhawks of the 3° Escuadrilla also participated in a joint exercise with the Brazilian Navy, Operation Fraterno, when they cooperated with Brazilian frigates *Defensora* (F41) and *Constituçáo* (F42).

On 10 September of that year, 3-A-302, 305, 207 and 312 were deployed to Rio Grande, because of a new increase in the tensions with Chile: three aircraft were kept on QRA during the following two weeks, one equipped with LAU-60 pods for unguided rockets, one with AIM-9B Sidewinders, and another with LAU-69 pods. As far as is known, there was only one occasion that any were scrambled: on 12 September 1980, the corvette ARA *Guerrico* (P32) detected a possible target and 3-A-302 and 3-A-305 scrambled although the contact

On 15 December 1978, 3-A-301 was scrambled by Captain Ítalo Lavezzo to intercept a Chilean Navy Casa C-212. The plane was armed with two AIM-9B Sidewinders.

A formation of eight A-4Qs seen shortly before the war, with aircraft 3-A-309, 314, 304, 302, 307, 305, 308 and 301.

Line of nine A-4Q Skyhawks shortly before the Malvinas/Falklands War.

was lost shortly after.

The last loss of any of COAN's A-4Q prior to the Falklands/Malvinas War took place on 9 August 1981, when 3-A-303 snapped wire number four while landing on board ARA 25 de Mayo: the aircraft rolled straight into the sea, the pilot managing to eject only once he was under the water – but survived his serious injuries.[4] Later

during the year the activity of the unit was reduced because many of its pilots were sent to France for conversion courses to the Dassault Super Etenard. Moreover, cracks were detected in the wings of some aircraft, resulting in leaks in integral fuel tanks, which grounded the entire fleet until the problem was fixed.

4

MOVING SOUTH

On 28 March 1982, four task forces of the Argentine Navy left Base Naval Puerto Belgrano with the aim of securing the Falkland Islands/Malvinas for Argentina and thus began Operation Rosario. The centrepiece of this effort was Task Group 79.1 (TG.79.1), with the aircraft carrier ARA 25 de Mayo (V-2), escorted by two Type 42 destroyers, Hercules and Santisima Trinidad. The aircraft assigned to the carrier embarked a day after TG.79.1 left Puerto Belgrano: these included four Grumman S-2E Trackers of Escuadrilla Aeronaval Antisubmarine (serials 2-AS-22, 2-AS-23, 2-AS-25, and 2-AS-26), and three A-4Q Skyhawks of 3° Escuadrilla (3-A-301, 3-A-305, and 3-A-314). One Sikorsky SH-3D Sea King (serial 2-H-234), and three Aerospatiale SE.316B Alouette III helicopters (serials 3-H-105, 3-H-111, and 3-H-112) were already on board.

The primary task of TG.79.1 was the provision of support for the main assault force. This consisted of the 2nd Marine Infantry Battalion, which was landed from the Landing Ship (Tank) Cabo San Antonio, together with one platoon of soldiers of the Army's 25th Infantry Regiment, on 2 April 1982. Two additional platoons of this regiment were embarked on the ice-breaker Almirante Irizar, which also carried two Coastguard helicopters, while other troops – including a party of combat swimmers and a 70-strong naval special forces group – were on board the submarine ARA Santa Fe, and the British-built Type 42 destroyer ARA Santisima Trinidad. Prior to the actual landing in the Falkland Islands /Malvinas, the Trackers flew multiple reconnaissance flights in their proximity, in order to make sure that no vessels of the Royal Navy were nearby. Instead, they found about 40 Polish and Soviet trawlers. The COAN Skyhawks did not take part in the landing because no close air support proved to be necessary.

3° Escuadrilla Works Up

After the landing operation, the A-4Qs which were embarked on the carrier returned to their base on 6 April and the personnel of 3° Escuadrilla began intensive training to prepare for war. Five pilots destined for other units were added to the unit, and five non-operational aircraft were returned to service – bringing the total of available airframes to eight – but two were in need of more extensive repairs (for an overview of available A-4Qs of 3° Escuadrilla at the time, see Table 3). Next, the unit exercised in-flight refuelling operations from the two KC-130Hs of the FAA, and that in cooperation with four out of five Dassault Super Etendards of 2° Escuadrilla. Furthermore, they ran exercises during which S-2Es guided them into simulated attacks on the two Type 42 destroyers of the Argentine Navy as these ships were similar to the ones operated by the Royal Navy. This resulted in several useful conclusions, one of which was that the Skyhawks had to descend to an altitude of less than 500ft whilst 100 miles (160km) away in order to remain undetected, and then descend to less than 100ft (30m) for the last 30 miles (48km) if they wanted to remain undetected by the radar. Once within visual range, they had to manoeuvre to avoid gunfire, and – during the actual bombing – had to be separated by more than 20 seconds from each other, in order to escape the debris from explosions caused by their own bombs.

During April, aircraft 3-A-301 and 306 received VLF Omega nav/attack systems, while another two were equipped with systems capable of receiving and analysing emissions from sonobuoys deployed by the Trackers: these were to serve as a VHF omni-direction range (VOR) navigational system under specific circumstances. 3° Escuadrilla embarked on ARA 25 de Mayo on 18 April again, this time with a total of eight aircraft and twelve pilots, and the ship sailed into the South Atlantic, with three A-4Qs standing quick reaction alert (or interceptor listo en cubierta, standing for 'interceptor ready on deck', ILC in Argentine Navy parlance):

• 1 armed with two AIM-9Bs to

A-4Qs of 3° Escuadrilla on the rear deck of ARA 25 de Mayo during Operation Rosario on 2 April 1982. Skyhawk 3-A-312 was lost on 21 May.

act as an interceptor;
- 1 armed for surface-attack and armed with a MER with six Mk.82 bombs under the centreline (all six Mk.82s were equipped with Mk.12 Snake Eye retarding fins), and
- 1 armed with chaff bombs.

Moreover, one aircraft – serial 3-A-302 – was equipped with a Sergeant Fletcher buddy-pack and prepared to act as a tanker. From then on until 27 April, the A-4Qs of 3° Escuadrilla flew reconnaissance north of the Falkland Islands/Malvinas, until TG.79.1 received the order to 'remain as a potential threat, and to operate when there is an opportunity.' In other words, TG.79.1 was to remain near the British-declared Total Exclusion Zone and wait for further developments.

Pilots of 3° Escuadrilla Aeronaval de Ataque at Río Grande during the war. In the back row: TF Márquez (killed in action), TN Lecour, RN Oliveira, CC Zubizarreta (killed during the war), CC Philippi, CC Castro Fox, TN Rótolo and TN Benítez. In the front row: TC Médici, TN Sylvester, TN Arca y TF Olmedo. (Photo archive CC Castro Fox)

Table 3: A-4Qs of 3° Escuadrilla, April-May 1982		
Serial	Callsign	Notes
0654	3-A-301	operational
0655	3-A-302	operational
0657	3-A-304	operational
0658	3-A-305	operational
0659	3-A-306	operational
0660	3-A-307	operational
0661	3-A-308	non-operational
0662	3-A-309	non-operational
0665	3-A-312	operational
0667	3-A-314	operational

The FAA's Organisation of the Battlefield

As of 1982, the FAA was commanded by Brigadier-General Basilio Arturo Ignacio Lami Dozo, who – together with Leopoldo Fortunato Galtieri and Jorge Isaac Anaya – was also a member of the 'National Reorganisation Process': the military junta that ruled Argentina from 1976 until 1983.[1] For operations in the zone of the disputed islands, Lami Dozo established the Fuerza Aérea Sur, commanded by Commando de la Fuerza Aérea Sud (CdoFAS). The post of the commander of the CdoFAS was assigned to the commander of IV Brigada Aérea and a Skyhawk-pilot, Brigadier-General Ernesto Horacio Crespo, who, with his staff, was to control all the aerial operations of the air force and during the following war. Many of the details about the composition and function of this command, or about its planning remain elusive: apparently, Crespo and his staff failed to develop a coherent strategy and were to order attacks only when they received information about the presence of British warships or ground troops at specific geographic positions.

The CdoFAS had its subordinated units deployed to a total of six air bases and airfields constructed at earlier times along the Argentine coast of the Atlantic Ocean. From north to south, these were:

- Base Aeronaval Almirante Zar (or BAAZ), Trelew
- IX Brigada Aérea of Comodoro Rivadavia
- BAM San Julián
- BAM Santa Cruz
- BAM Rio Gallegos, and
- Base Aeronaval Almirante Quijada (BAAQ), Río Grande

The only paved runway on the disputed islands – the one at Port Stanley – was found to be unsuitable for fast jet operations. The FAA did decide to extend the local runway by using aluminium plates, but the war erupted before the necessary materials and construction equipment could be dispatched to the islands. Therefore, the local airfield – dubbed BAM Malvinas by the Argentines – was used only by transport aircraft. Furthermore, the Argentines developed two further airfields for use by its lighter aircraft: the one at Pebble Island was named Estación Aeronaval Calderón, and the one at Goose Green was called BAM Cóndor . That said, the FAA did manage to deploy its 2nd Early Warning and Control Group (Grupo 2 Vigilancia y Control Aereo) and to construct a combat information centre (Centro de Information y Control, CIC) and a fighter-control station (Estacion de Interceptacion, EI) on the disputed islands. Supported by one AN/TPS-43 and one AN/TPS-44 radar, each with a range of about 150 miles (241km), the CIC and the EI coordinated the operations of interceptors, fighter-bombers, and ground-based air defences.

Escuadrón I Aeromóvil: IV Brigada's Deployment

The first Skyhawk-equipped unit to come under the control of CdoFAS was Escuadrón 1 de Cazabombardeo of Group 4 de Caza: this had five of its 17 A-4C Skyhawks deployed at BAM Rio Gallegos for Operation Gélido II, which was – as explained earlier – part of the rotational deployment of the FAA's fighter-bomber units in the wake of the crisis with Chile. Although available, they did not take part in the 2 April operations. By the time the main fighting began on 1 May 1982, the unit had four escadrilles, each with five pilots, four of whom were ready for combat, and one was a student. The aircraft at Río Gallegos were C-302, C-309, C-310, C-324 and C-325 and were the first aircraft of the unit to participate in training missions within the theatre of operations.

Understanding that the mass of its pilots possessed no experience

An A-4C flies low over BAM Malvinas in April 1982.

An A-4C passes over BAM Malvinas during the
first flights over the islands in April 1982.

A Skyhawk taxiing after a mission at BAM San Julián.

The apron at San Julián, with four A-4Bs, one Aerocommander 500U,
one Hughes 500 and a Bell 212 of the Chaco province government.

A Skyhawk at BAM San Julián, armed with a single Mk.17
bomb. The Mk.17 was only used during the first days of the
war: later on, it was replaced with EXPAL BR.250 bombs.

An A-4C, seen refuelling from a KC-130H early
during the war, armed with an Mk.17 bomb.

Mario Caffarati), C-309 (Alférez Carlos Codrington), C-310 (Captain Záttara), and C-324 (PT Vázquez) took off from Río Gallegos and flew over the islands and the airfield of Port Stanley (re-named as BAM Malvinas by the Argentines). On the following day the mission was repeated by aircraft C-309, C-310, C-324 and C-325, so the pilots could familiarise themselves with the operations theatre.

The A-4Cs deployed at San Julián were officially organised into a provisional unit named Escuadron 1 Aeromóvil Although a civil facility, this already had eight bunkers for the protection of combat aircraft, and a runway extended with aluminium plates, and connected to the Route 3 highway, where the aircraft could be dispersed. As of March 1982, and in expectation to serve as a major forward air base in the event of a war with Chile, San Julián further received an air traffic control centre supported by one AN/TPS-44 early warning radar, was protected by anti-aircraft artillery and received bunkers for ground personnel. Correspondingly, nearly all of the crews deployed there knew this installation very well, and – when ordered to deploy there as the tensions with the United Kingdom began to rise – most of the crews planned their stay in the municipal hotel in the nearby town. The ferry flight from Mendoza was made with the support of a C-130H Hercules and Boeing 707 serial TC-93. Four aircraft from Río Gallegos and six from Mendoza transferred to the new base on 10 April, while another followed two days later. By 1 May 1982, CdoFAS had under its control the A-4Cs listed in Table 4, and the number of A-4B and A-4C Skyhawks listed in Table 5.

in operations over the high seas, the CdoFAS issued an order for all units to undertake as many familiarisation flights over the islands as possible. Correspondingly, on 5 April 1982, C-302 (with Captain

Table 4: A-4Cs of Escuadron 1 Aeromóvil, BAM Río Gallegos, April-May 1982	
Version	Serial
A-4C	C-302
A-4C	C-303
A-4C	C-304
A-4C	C-309
A-4C	C-310
A-4C	C-313
A-4C	C-318
A-4C	C-319

Anti-Ship Training

The A-4Cs of IV Brigada Aérea resumed their overflights of the disputed islands on 13 April 1982: three days later the unit went as far as to not only send its Skyhawks over the Malvinas again, but also to run live-firing exercises with 20mm internal cannon for aircraft C-304, C-313, C-319, and C-325. Meanwhile, back at Mendoza, ground crews returned the VLF Omega navigational systems to service on six aircraft – including C-314, C-319, C-320 and C-321. On 21 April, gun tests were also made with C-318 and repeated on the following day with the same aircraft. Gerardo Isaac, who wore the rank of an Alférez at the time, recalled:

… any ship that went by we took off and made simulated attacks, tankers, trawlers, navy vessels. We practiced different types of tactics to attack ships, which we knew how it was, we had advice from the navy. The advice of the navy was important but then we adopted another system, after having studied the formations and having worked a lot with the Skyguard radar of antiaircraft artillery for both the Roland and 35mm guns. We came to the conclusion that the best formation was the line attack, more or less between 50 and 100 meters between aircraft and that was a good tactic so that the radar had doubts which target to engage. If we had been staggered with some differences in depth or breadth, we would probably get engaged and the radar had time to engage the next, but when we were in that line formation we went to see the radar and the radar would jump from one aircraft to the other and couldn't engage any target.

On the 23rd, the last flight over the islands was made by Skyhawks C-313 and C-325, while training flights over the sea took place with the remaining aircraft. Finally, on 25 April, a horizontal bombing exercise was flown utilizing C-304 and C-322. A typical bomb load used during the war consisted of three Argentine-made, parachute-retarded, Explosivos Alaveses BRP.250 bombs.[2] From 11 May, the unit also began deploying British-made 1,000lb (500kg) Mk.17 bombs, but this practice was abandoned once the Argentines realised that these tended to crash all the way through the targeted ships

without detonating (as in the case of HMS *Glasgow*, D88, on 12 May 1982). Isaac continued:

I remember the delay of the fuses varied and at the end of the war [it] was at 12 seconds. The 500-pounders gave a bigger guarantee that they ended in the ship and would not fly through and exit on the other side. After the war the armament analysis continued, we saw that lower weight bombs would have been better. Experimentation was made during the 45 days of real conflict from May 1 to June 14 so we ended up with 3 bombs of 500 pounds without a parachute, with two fuses and with 12 seconds of delay, sometimes 6.

Four days later, because of an alert for a possible British bombing over mainland bases, four A-4Cs were sent to Base Aeronaval Comandante Espora (BACE) armed with Shafrir missiles, to act as interceptors. This was necessary because the COAN aircraft were deployed on board ARA *25 de Mayo* and no other aircraft were available. On 1 May, the unit fired its first Shafrir Mk.2 air-to-air missiles in an exercise, as Isaac explained:

On April 29 there was an air raid warning to the base. At night there were few people left, most had gone to the town hall, but there was still my escadrille, Garcia, Farias, Casco and me. The Chief of Operations, I think it was Perondi, told us that we had to go to the shelters to take off with the A-4s heading north, because there was [the] threat of imminent air attack. We had an anecdote of an error from us. In April the radio frequencies were changed every day. At night the frequencies for the next day arrived, then when the activity ended we would grab the list, erase the ones from the day and set the frequency for the next day. We had already done it, we went to the end of the runway to take off, we could not communicate with the tower, so we got on the runway end to the east to take off to the west and while we were giving power to take off three M5 Daggers took off from the other side, and went through the middle of our formation. Once they had passed, we took off and headed north, the order we had was to communicate with Comodoro Rivadavia, it was a mother frequency that was always the same. So we communicated and they passed us the coordinates of where we had to go and it was Comandante Espora Naval Aviation Base. When we arrived we expected a Vicecomodoro who was the link to CATOS, with the Navy. CATOS was the aerial command of the southern theatre of operations, which was the air commander for the conflict with Chile. It was still organised, the southern air force was not created

The A-4Cs C-309 and 313 as seen at Mendoza, shortly before the war – in the course of which both were to be shot down.

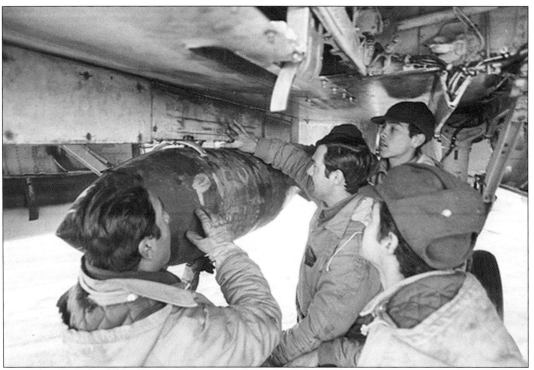

A rare view of a ground crew installing a British-made Mk.17 bomb under the centreline pylon.

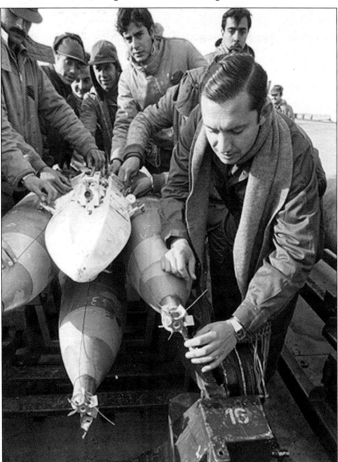

Weapons specialists setting fuses on three
BR.250 bombs mounted on a TER.

me, we are all officers in the air force', the guy explained to him and started to raise the temperature of the discussion until at the end we all went to sleep at 'Michela'. We passed the 30th with bad weather in San Julián and we could not go back.

Escuadrón II Aeromóvil: V Brigada's Deployment

Meanwhile, similar preparations were also underway within V Brigada Aérea. Marcelo Moroni, who wore the rank of an Alférez at the time, recalled:

2 April found us in Villa Reynolds. That morning, the brigade commander informed us that the islands had been taken, and that, according to the political forecasts, the United Nations would intervene. The oldest, worried about the situation, asked that foreseeing all this we must bring people from the Navy to advise us on the issues of weapons, capabilities, attack modes, tactics, to see how we defined this issue and how training should develop from there. A few days later, we received a visit from a naval aviator – a frigate captain – from the Navy, who told us a lot about the capacity of the fleet and the capacity of certain warships of the British fleet.

A week later, V Brigada Aérea received an order for the deployment of A-4B Skyhawks of its Grupo 5 de Caza to BAM Río Gallegos, where these were to form Escuadrón II Aeromóvil. BAM Rio Gallegos was a fully developed military air base, including the local air traffic control centre, and was to see the deployment of numerous other units of the air force and the navy during the war.

V Brigada's first flight to the islands – a reconnaissance – was undertaken by a single A-4B on 13 April and then by a pair two days later. That said, the subsequent development of this unit was slow in comparison to that of the A-4Cs: on 16 April, another pair made a training sortie flying at low altitude close to Río Gallegos, and a day later two A-4Bs were re-deployed from Villa Reynolds to the southern base. On the same day – 17 April 1982 – two Skyhawks of Escuadrón II Aeromóvil escorted a Canberra bomber on an anti-ship training mission, flying low over 200 miles away from the mainland. Further flights over the islands were undertaken on 19 and 22 April. According to Moroni, pre-war studies had shown that only two out of every eight aircraft attacking the Royal Navy's warships would be expected return from their mission. Therefore, the pilots subsequently flew intensive low-altitude training sessions against the wreck of SS *Marjory Glenn* off the coast of Punta Loyola, near Río Gallegos. All attacks were performed from the sea, and with an observer monitoring results.

On 23 April, three additional aircraft were transferred to Río Gallegos, while another flight made a test flight to the islands, which was repeated two days later. On 27 April, five further aircraft arrived at Río Gallegos, but another three were sent back to Villa Reynolds on the 29th: thus, Grupo 5 entered the war with 24 A-4Bs available.

By 2 May, Escuadrón II Aeromóvil had 10 A-4Bs at BAM Río

yet. He asked us what we needed, we went to the hotel, CATOS was paying so we opened the menu, we ordered the most expensive and we had two bottles of San Felipe wine. We returned to the base, the officer told us, about the lodging: 'the officers are going to the officers' casino and the Alférez is going to go to the 'Michela' (where the midshipmen were staying). Garcia looks at him and says 'excuse

The wreck of *Marjory Glenn* – used as a target for anti-ship exercises by A-4Bs and A-4Cs of the FAA.

Gallegos – including three jets (flown by Captitan Antoio Zelaya, PT Fausto Gavazzi and Alférez Guillermo Dellepiane) that had already arrived there on 23 April. Teniente Mario Roca (who retired with the rank of Brigadier), recalled:

We landed in Trelew and there we had the first visual contact with the reality of the war. They went to look for us, they took us in a vehicle that I think was from the Canberra squadron, to what was supposed to be the air group, and in the middle of the darkness we saw a Canberra that had a broken wing, it was one of those that had returned, which had a missile detonated near the tip of the wing and had broken it. There we made contact with real life. We went to Operations where the Canberra squadron was. At dawn we took off from Trelew to Río Gallegos, knowing that the weather in Río Gallegos was very poor. I went with the flight of Varela, Moroni, Mayor and me. …the first day of the war was on 1 May, when we experienced such issues as the attack on the ELMA *Formosa* and our first losses. A hellish day for everyone, an anxiety and an important stress, in that you had to eat, sleep and organise.

The weapons deployed to BAM Río Gallegos for the use on A-4Bs were similar to those deployed by A-4Cs: 250kg BR.250s – with both

Pilots of Grupo 5 de Caza (V Brigada Aérea) with journalists inside their ready room.

The pilots of Escuadrón II Aeromóvil waiting for another mission.

A pilot of V Brigada Aérea about to board his A-4B, while ground crews wait to power-up the engine.

Captain Carballo explaining a mission to Brigadier-General Basilio Lami Dozo, commander of the FAA.

conventional fins and in the parachute-retarded variant (BRP.250) – and British-made Mk.17 1,000lbs bombs were in use from 11 May.

Table 5: A-4s assigned to the CdoFAS as of 1 May 1982	
Base	Number of Aircraft and Unit
San Julián	8 A-4C from VI Brigada Aérea, operated as Escuadron I Aeromóvil
Río Gallegos	22 A-4B from V Brigada Aérea, operated as Escuadrón II Aeromóvil

5
DEADLY SKIRMISHING

Early on 1 May 1982, a steady stream of reports about British airstrikes and naval bombardments of airfields on the disputed islands reached CdoFAS. 'Putting all the meat on the Grill,' as the Argentines tend to say, Brigadier-General Crespo and his staff promptly issued orders for a massive deployment of almost all of the available aircraft over the disputed islands. The Argentine Skyhawks thus became involved in their first major armed conflict.

An Unpromising Start
One of CdoFAS's first operational orders – OF.1092 – resulted in the scramble of Topo Flight of Escuadrón II Aeromóvil. This included Capitán Hugo Palaver (A-4B serial number C-244), TT Daniel Gálvez (C-206), PT Luciano Guadagnini (C-221) and Alférez Hugo Gómez (C-225). They refuelled from a KC-130 and arrived over the islands, but then the ground control confused them with a combat air patrol of FAA Mirages and vectored them to intercept a pair of Sea Harriers. The pilots realised the mistake when noticing the altitude of their assigned target and requested help as the Royal Navy's interceptors were now approaching them. The ground control then dispatched Tablón Flight of Mirage IIIEAs, and the Sea Harriers abandoned their chase. The first combat sortie of V Brigada Aérea thus ended with all four Skyhawks landing back at BAM Río Gallegos at 12:00.

Escuadrón I Aeromóvil went into action only minutes later. OF.1095 sent Oro Flight into action from San Julián, including four A-4Cs each armed with two BRP.250s for an anti-ship strike. The

Alférez Hugo Gómez in C-225, refuelling from a KC-130H during the 1 May mission, when he flew with Topo Flight.

formation, including Capitán Castellano (C-322), TT Paredi (C-318), Capitán Caffarati (C-319), and TT Lucero (C-302), got airborne at 11:00. After refuelling in the air from a KC-130H, it reached the islands, but found no target and returned at 13:30. Ten minutes earlier, Pampa Flight had taken-off, including PT José Vazquez (C-304) and TT Atilio Záttara (C-304), each armed with a pair of Sharfir Mk.2s. Following the obligatory refuelling from a KC-130H, the pair reached the islands, but the FAA's CIC could not find any suitable targets for them. Isaac's recollection of the day was as follows:

Lt. Daniel Gálvez in C-206 leaving the KC-130H which refuelled him en route to the islands on 1 May 1982 when he was part of Topo Flight.

Two A-4Cs, seen from a KC-130H tanker, en route to a mission.

An A-4C Armed with 500lb (250kg) BR.250 bombs approaches a KC-130H to refuel during an attack sortie.

Having outboard underwing pylons, the A-4Cs were capable of carrying three BR.250s installed on these and on the centreline hardpoint instead of all three on the TER (a configuration that created slightly more drag). This example was photographed while refuelling from a KC-130H on 1 May 1982.

A-4C serial C-302, piloted by Lucero, as seen during refuelling from a KC-130H, on 1 May 1982, underway for its first combat sortie of the war.

On May 1, García went to the flight plan office to check the weather in San Julián and when he came back, he told us that we were going to return because at 04:40 they attacked Puerto Argentino and the weather will improve. We went to San Julián Airport, the weather was better, when we were starting to descend in San Julián we heard that Daggers and A-4Cs had gone out for air defence and air patrol missions and when we arrived they told us: 'go eat, as it is feasible that on return there is a mission that will be assigned to you.' We went to the city and came back and they gave us an attack mission against the ships that were bombing Puerto Argentino.

Indeed, at 14:00, another pair of A-4Cs launched, including TT Néstor López (C-303) and PT Daniel Manzotti (C-310): once again, they found no targets and returned to base safely. Finally, the third air superiority mission – Pampa Flight – was launched from San Julián at 15:20, including Capitán Almoño (C-322) and Alférez Codrington (C-325): due to communication problems during the IFR-operation both aircraft returned to their base early, thus ending the last mission of IV Brigada Aérea during which the A-4Cs carried the Shafrir Mk.2 missiles. The reason for this decision was that the FAA concluded that the A-4C with older Shafir Mk.II missiles was inferior to the Sea Harrier FRS.Mk 1 armed with US-made AIM-9L Sidewinder missiles.[1]

Because of further reports about Royal Navy activity along the coast of the disputed islands, at 16:00 CdoFAS ordered additional formations into the air. Trueno Flight of Escuadrón II Aeromóvil launched from Río Gallegos under operational order OF.1110, including Captain Pablo Carballo (C-215), TT Carlos Rinke (C-212), PT Carlos Cachón (C-225), and Alférez Leonardo Carmona (C-240). When they arrived at the islands they could not find any targets and thus turned back west. However, while passing the southern part of San Carlos Sound, they saw a ship and attacked at 17:45. The leader hit the vessel with his guns and a bomb – which failed to detonate – while another A-4B hit one of the ship's cranes and it fell into the sea. All aircraft returned to base safely, only for their pilots to be informed that they had attacked the Argentine merchant ELMA *Formosa*, which was returning to the mainland without unloading all of her cargo.

At 16:29, Foca Flight took off under OF.1112, with Captain Carlos Varela leading TT Mario Roca, but the two Skyhawks were ordered to return shortly after reaching the archipelago due to the presence of a Royal Navy CAP. Only a minute behind them was another flight (launched under OF.1113), including PT Mariano Velasco (C-206), TT Carlos Ossés (C-246) and PT Héctor Sánchez (C-209). The last had to abort due to technical issues, while the others found no targets to attack.

Meanwhile, OF.1114 prompted the launch of Lana Flight, including Capitán Garcia (C-318), TT Casco (C-319), Alférez Isaac (C-309), and TT Farias (C-302). Isaac recalled:

We planned the mission, we took off, we did air refueling, we descended, we got low before arriving at San Carlos Bay, we entered from the south due east towards the Isla Del Águila and there we continued over the land to the area of Puerto Argentino, as it was planned. When we were about to arrive at San Carlos Strait/ Falkland Sound, although we did not listen to the radar operator, we heard the communication chaos that was in the air, that they

Cachón, Barrionuevo, Carmona and Velasco at San Julián.

C-224 being prepared for a mission at Río Gallegos.

The A-4B flown by Captain Palaver seen while refuelling from a KC-130H on 1 May 1982, when he was part of Topo Flight. On 25 May Palaver would be shot down by a Sea Dart from HMS *Coventry*, shortly before the destroyer was sunk by Mariano Velasco and his A-4B.

to base', we did not know who it was and we keep flying, for the second time he tells us the same thing and we keep flying, for the third time the same voice saying once again clearly that the radar was ordering us to turn 180° and return to the base, so we obeyed without knowing to whom. We turned, we ejected charges, bombs and tanks, and we went back to San Julián without knowing who had spoken to us. We landed in San Julián, the rest of those who had left to fly had returned, of which there was the Dagger escadrille of Dimeglio, Román and Aguirre Faget, that was the one that attacked the *Glamorgan*, the *Arrow* and the *Alacrity*. They were part of the Dagger squadron that was in San Julián. When we came to Operations they were watching the films of the Dagger's camera. They were all happy, basically because they had been successful attacks, they did not shoot down anyone from our base, it was all euphoria until the afternoon, when information from the other bases began to arrive and then we learned that they shot down Ardiles (Dagger), Ibañez with Gómez (Canberra), Perona and García Cuerva (Mirage III), so that on May 1, at the end of the day we learned the reality that we in San Julián had not yet experienced. But doubt remained, they looked at us sideways asking 'these, why did they come back?'. On May 3 there was a meeting in Comodoro Rivadavia called by the Southern Air Force commander. Brigadier Crespo summoned the escadrille leaders who had flown on May 1 to determinate the lessons learned and modify some behaviours to improve discipline in flight. When Garcia returned, he met us and told us that the most important thing was that when we were in the middle of the meeting, Captain Carballo (pilot of an A-4B) got up and asked who were the Lana on May 1, Garcia tells him that we were and Carballo said 'three times I told you to turn back, you had a Sea Harrier patrol six miles ahead that was about to intercept you, if you had not returned they were going to shoot you down.' So somehow he cleaned up our stain, because there were some who would not believe us and he made it clear in front of everyone.

Waiting and Calculating

Meanwhile, the Argentine Navy attempted to bring its TG.79.1 into action: informed about the approach of the Royal Navy's task force from the north-eastern direction, the carrier battle group moved into

were telling everything that was happening to each one, the one that saw the Canberra crew that had ejected, the other one who had seen a ship, it was a mess. We continued our course because the radar did not contact us anymore. When we were over the strait somebody calls us and says 'Lana turn 180°, you have to go back

Ground crew with A-4B C-212 of Escuadrón II Aeromóvil (V Brigada Aérea), at Río Gallegos, later during the war. Notable are two kill markings applied directly below the serial number on the forward fuselage. (Santiago Rivas Collection)

ELMA *Formosa*, attacked by mistake on 1 May.

ELMA *Río Carcarañá*.

attack, and the personnel of 3° Escuadrilla were ordered to prepare for action.

Within the squadron, the decision was taken to ready six aircraft, that would carry a total of 24 Mk.82 bombs between them: the calculation was that only four might reach the target, but out of 16 bombs they would have released, at least 25% (i.e. 4) would hit their target – thus probably neutralising at least one of the Royal Navy's carriers. Even if only two A-4Qs were likely to return from such a mission, this was concluded to be worth trying.

The Almost-Carrier Battle

At 17:28, another Tracker was launched from *25 de Mayo* with the task of finding the British fleet. However, the aircraft developed problems while overflying a group of Soviet trawlers, and could only detect strong radar emissions, without finding their source, even while continuing well to the east. Nevertheless, 3° Escuadrilla prepared its strike force and pilots Capitán de Corbeta (CC) Alberto Philippi, Teniente de Fragata (TF) Márquez, Tenientes de Navío (TNs) Olmedo, José César Arca and Lecour, and Teniente de Corbeta (TC) Medici remained on alert. The distance to their target was expected to be more than 200 miles (321km), which was well beyond the range of A-4Qs armed with six Mk.82 (150 miles or 241km). Therefore, ARA *25 de Mayo* turned east to cut down the range. Before long however, it became obvious that the ship could not reach a suitable position for the launch of her aircraft before sunset, and the Skyhawks were not equipped for a nocturnal anti-ship strike.

a position north-west of the islands, waiting for its opportunity.[2]

On 1 May, around 15:13, Tracker 2-AS-23 detected seven ships that were considered 'British' at position 49°34' S/57°10' W. Minutes later, an aircraft was detected by the main radar of ARA *25 de Mayo*, and the sole A-4Q interceptor was scrambled. The target in question turned out to have been Canberra bombers of the FAA returning from a fruitless attack mission. Nevertheless, the presence of unknown ships in the east was considered a good opportunity for an anti-ship

Thus, at 18:00, TG.79.1 turned south and sailed a zig-zag course, while Tracker 2-AS-26 was prepared for another reconnaissance sortie.

At 23:00, the latter made another contact, this time at 50°00' S/56°25' W. 3° Escuadrilla was alerted for action – this time at dawn – and the pilots were briefed for the mission (for a list of pilots and aircraft selected for what could have become a historic first carrier battle since 1945, see Table 6). Another A-4Q was kept as a reserve, and one prepared as a tanker.

The launch of the strike was expected to take place at 06:00 on 2 May. However, additional reconnaissance sorties by S-3Es failed to find the enemy warships. Moreover, although the decision was taken to launch the Skyhawks anyway, there were only 10 knots of wind, while the bomb-loaded A-4Qs needed 40 knots for a successful catapult launch. Thus, the first ever carrier battle since the Second World War was effectively prevented by weather that was entirely unusual for the South Atlantic at this time of the year.

Table 6: A-4Qs and Pilots of the 3° Escuadrilla prepared for Anti-Ship Strike on 1-2 May 1982	
Callsign	Pilot
3-A-301	CC Castro Fox
3-A-314	TF Márquez
3-A-302	TN Benítez
3-A-306	TN Oliveira
3-A-312	TN Lecour
3-A-305	TN Sylvester

The Withdrawal of TG.79.1
Although no anti-ship attack was launched, two A-4Qs were kept on a 5-minute alert, while the six bomb-laden aircraft were kept on a 30-minute alert. At 09:00, an alert was sounded after an unidentified aircraft was detected well to the south-east, and CC Philippi was scrambled in 3-A-304 (TC Medici in 3-A-307 had to abort the scramble due to technical failures), though no intercept took place. The same was true for another alert, sounded at 11:00, when TF Márquez was scrambled in A-4Q 3-A-307, followed by CC Castro Fox in 3-A-304. Neither of the pilots found anything, and the ultimate conclusion was that that the detected targets were FAA aircraft returning to the mainland.

Ultimately, following the sinking of the cruiser ARA *General Belgrano* (C-5), TG.79.1 received the order to cancel its attack. Still,

two interceptors – 3-A-304 and 3-A-307 – were kept on 5-minute alert with pilots in the cockpit, and the six bomb-laden attack aircraft on a 3-hour alert, even as of the morning of 3 May. All further expectations for possible action disappeared at 13:30, when Task Force 79.1 received the order to withdraw from the war zone: Royal Navy nuclear attack submarine HMS *Spartan* (S105) was suspected nearby, representing much too serious a threat for the flagship of the Argentine Navy. Moving directly for the coast, and then close to it towards the north, TG.79.1, the carrier and its two escorts, evaded detection by the Royal Navy and withdrew safely to Puerto Belgrano. For all of that time, no fewer than four A-4Qs – serials 3-A-304, 3-A-307, 3-A-312, and 3-A-314 – were kept on alert as interceptors, and the other four as bombers.

Indeed, during the afternoon of 3 May, another air raid warning was sounded, and CC Philippi (3-A-304) and TC Medici (3-A-307) catapulted into the air, but only found air force aircraft. The last alert of the day prompted the launch of CC Zubizarreta (3-A-304), TF Olmedo (3-A-307), and TN Lecour (3-A-314) – though with exactly the same result.

On 9 May, all eight A-4Q Skyhawks of 3° Escuadrilla were launched from ARA *25 de Mayo* for a transfer flight to Base Aeronaval Comandante Espora. Three days later, the aircraft and their crews were temporarily deployed to Base Aeronaval Contraalmirante Quijada outside Río Grande. However, by then four aircraft had developed technical malfunctions and had to return to Comandante Espora: it was only on 14 May that all returned to Contraalmirante Quijada, and the unit was complete again. From the next day, six A-4Qs were kept on alert, all armed with four Mk.82s; another one acted as reserve, and one as a tanker. Their pilots were organised into two flights:
- CC Castro Fox, TC Medici, TN Benitez, CC Zubizarreta, TN Olmedo and TN Oliveira
- CC Philippi, TF Marquez, TN Arca, TN Rótolo, TN Lecour, and TN Sylvester.

In the course of an accident related to an attempt to start the engine of 3-A-302 on 18 May, the only available buddy-pack was damaged and the IFR-capability lost. Thus, the unit was henceforth dependent upon cooperation with the FAA's two KC-130Hs, just like the air force's own Skyhawks. Certainly enough, 3-A-302 and its buddy-tank were repaired two days later, and meanwhile CC Philippi and TC Medici ran a test-sortie during which they refuelled from the Super Etendard flown by CC Curilovic. However, for unknown reasons, this kind of sortie was never flown in earnest.

A Period of Bad Weather
With the withdrawal of TG.79.1, the emphasis on Argentine Skyhawk-operations over the Islas Malvinas fell to the assets under the control of the FAA's CdoFAS. The complement of Escuadrón II Aeromóvil at Río Gallegos was completed with arrival of additional A-4Bs on 2

A pair of Snakeye-tailed Mk.82s mounted at the rear of a MER laying on a trolley waiting to be loaded aboard an A-4Q. To the rear is an A-4Q parked near the island of the aircraft carrier ARA *25 de Mayo*. Notable is the name of HMS *Invincible* inscribed on the upper bomb by one of the ground crew. Photograph taken on the afternoon of 1 May 1982.

May, but most of the pilots spent the day listening to instructions from pilots of Escadrón I Aeromóvil that already had significant experience in flying over the disputed islands. Another issue of interest was the search for ways to improve communication with the CIC and the EI on the Malvinas, so as to avoid mistakes like the one that happened to Topo Flight. Moroni recalled: 'There we started flying interspersed: the unit that was on leave had a flight on alert in the case the duty-squadron was all airborne, or if it received so-called fragmentary orders.'

On 18 May 1982 3-A-302 had an accident when the nosewheel collapsed. Despite the aircraft being quickly repaired, the buddy pack being carried, the only operational one, remained out of service for the rest of the war.

Escuadrón II Aeromóvil planned a large-scale attack for 3 May against ships detected close to the islands, and CdoFAS issued the corresponding fragmentary orders OF.1150 and OF.1151. Fiera Flight – including A-4Bs flown by Captain Carballo, PT Velasco, TT Sergio Mayor and Alférez Alfredo Vázquez – took off at 15:53, and was followed by Trueno Flight, including Capitán Palaver, PT Cachón, TT Rinke and Alférez Gómez, just two minutes later. However, before they could reach the islands, both formations were

An A-4C taking off from BAM San Julián with three BR.250 bombs on a Triple Ejector Rack (TER) and early-war style identification markings in yellow.

recalled: it turned out the ships were Argentine. A similar situation developed on 6 May, when CdoFAS wanted to launch an all-out attack on the Royal Navy's aircraft carriers. Correspondingly, OF.1168 and OF.1169 prompted Escuadrón II Aeromóvil to prepare Fiera and Trueno flights of four A-4Bs each. Moreover, Tejo Flight of A-4Cs was to depart together with Barón Flight of four A-4Bs and four Daggers of Chango Flight. However, the Argentines could not find any of the British warships and thus no sortie was launched. Instead, the pilots returned to flying training sorties against the wreck of SS *Marjory Glenn*.

Meanwhile, there was no activity at San Julián on 2 May, although Escuadrón I Aeromóvil developed a plan for attacks against various ground and naval targets. On 3 May CdoFAS order OF.1152 required a mission by Oso Flight (aircraft C-302, C-303, C-318, and C-325), armed with three BRPs each, starting at 16:07. They were followed fifteen minutes later by Dogo Flight (OF.1153) with aircraft C-304, 309 and 310 armed with the same weapons. After refuelling from KC-130H TC-69 they found no targets and returned to San Julián at 17:18.

On 4 May a new aircraft joined the squadron, with the arrival of C-314 from Área de Material Río IV. Additional sorties were planned: for example, OF.1170 ordered Tejo Flight into action with four A-4Cs that launched on 6 May 1982 at 16:45 to strike a naval target positioned at 51°08'S/62°27'W. However, the pilots found nothing. Furthermore, CdoFAS devised a plan for the case that the Royal Navy's carrier battle group entered the operational range of the FAA's aircraft, and

Alférez Schwind, Alférez "Toba" Nieto, Capitán Carballo and Teniente "Tom" Lucero (of Grupo 4 de Caza). The aircraft is armed with an AN M65 454kg bomb with Mk.17 tail, locally called "Bombola."

intended to react with a massive airstrike: this was to start with two flights (Cobra and Pitón) of Daggers from Río Grande (OF.1181 and OF.1182), followed by six flights of A-4s: three of these (Toro, Gloster and Palo operating under OF.1183-1187) were to include a total of eight A-4Cs from San Julián armed with Mk.17s, while the others (Tejo, Morro and Mate, operating according to OF.1188-1190) were to

Mechanics saluting the pilot of A-4B serial number C-242 as it rolls out for the next combat sortie.

include A-4Bs. Thirty minutes later, three additional flights of A-4Bs (Nene, Oso, and Puma, operating along OF.1191-1193) were to deliver the final blow. However, the combination of bad weather, the poor Argentine capability to run reconnaissance around the islands, and the fact that the Royal Navy's task force did not approach, resulted in the cancellation of this plan.

9 May: First Losses

Bad weather kept most of the FAA's aircraft grounded until 9 May, when the FAA's CIC on the disputed islands reported the presence of the destroyer HMS *Coventry* (D118) and the frigate HMS *Broadsword* (F88) detected about 40 miles north of Port Stanley/Puerto Argentino. Dubbed the 'Type 64' or '42-22 combo' by the Royal Navy, this combination represented a major obstacle for Argentine fighter-bombers. The destroyer was equipped to detect enemy aircraft and engage them at range out to 74 kilometres (46 miles) with help of the GWS-30 Sea Dart surface-to-air missile system; the frigate was equipped with the GWS-25 Sea Wolf automated point-defence weapon system to protect the destroyer and itself.[3]

CdoFAS promptly reacted by issuing OF.1174, which ordered Trueno Flight – including Capitán Garcia (C-310), TT Farias (C-303), TT Casco (C-313), and Alférez Isaac (C-322) – into action. Isaac recalled:

We had a mission to attack a ship to the north of the Malvinas in the open sea. We took off the four of us and went to refuel. My

section leader was Casco and the flight-leader was Garcia. I was 4 and Farías was 2, he was one of those who had come from Pucará and we finished the training together. When we were doing inflight refuelling, I was on the right hose of the KC-130. Casco, who was in observation on the right, told me 'stay formed because I want to see something', I stayed on the hose, Casco went down, formed next to me and said 'a piece of your airplane flew away', so I returned to the base and Garcia had failure in refuelling. We both went back to San Julián and Casco and Farías followed. There was very bad weather, with low ceiling and rain in the whole area of the islands, there was already a relay to improve the discipline of communications, a Learjet that was at 35,000 to 40,000 feet. They were reporting to the squadrons what was happening and they were all reporting that they were not making contact with the ground due to bad weather, they descended and started to return. All the squadrons turned back – except for Casco and Farías. The relay, seeing everything that was happening, called Casco to ask about his situation and Casco said back something like 'do not break my balls, I'm with 50 meters of ceiling and 50 of visibility'. That was the last thing he said and they did not come back. The return time passed, we went to the tower, we called all the bases, we stayed all night, we did not know what had happened, although a very strong hypothesis was an accident, that they had crashed into an island or the water, but we did not know it until quite some time later.

Flying underneath the cloud ceiling of a mere 300ft and thus in low visibility conditions, the pilots called the radar operator at Port Stanley/Puerto Argentino, who stated the targets were to the east of the town. The pilots said they didn't have any reference to their location, because they couldn't see the islands, while the FAA's AN/TPS-43 could not track them because of their low altitude to the northwest of the islands. After that, contact was lost. It was only years later that the Argentines found out what happened to the two pilots of the IV Brigade Aérea that day. Ultimately, the wreckage of A-4C C-313 was found on South Jason Island: the aircraft hit the ground while moving from west towards east. No trace was ever found of C-303: that Skyhawk probably hit the sea close to the island, as both Skyhawks disappeared around the same time.

Despite all the aborts caused by the bad weather, IV Brigada Aérea did launch two additional missions on 9 May 1982: at 14:15, Cóndor Flight took off under OF.1177, including

An A-4C on its way to the Malvinas, armed with one Mk.17 bomb under the centreline, refuelling from a KC-130H Hercules.

Capitán Mario Caffarati (C-318), PT José Vázquez (C-325) and TT Ricardo Lucero (C-309). This was followed by Fortin Flight (OF.1178), including PT Ureta (C-304) and TT Paredi (C-319). Disturbed by bad weather, none of them found any kind of target: Cóndor Flight returned at 16:50, and Fortin at 17:30.

12 May: Second Clash with the 'Type 64'

With the CIC reporting the appearance of the destroyer HMS *Glasgow* (D88) and the frigate HMS *Brilliant* (F90) north of the islands again, on 12 May 1982 CdoFAS issued OF.1177, following which both the A-4Cs of Escuadrón I Aeromóvil and A-4Bs of Escuadrón II Aeromóvil were sent into action. At 12:20, the latter launched Cuña Flight, including PT Manuel Bustos (C-246), TTs Jorge Iberlucea (C-208), Mario Nívoli (C-206), and Alférez Alfredo Vázquez (C-242). After refuelling, they reached the Falklands/Malvinas flying at a very low altitude, until finding their targets off Port Stanley. Accelerating to maximum speed, the formation split into two pairs, each flying in line abreast, as planned. HMS *Glasgow* picked up the incoming Skyhawks with its Type 909 radar, but the Sea Dart system malfunctioned: as the range closed, the ship trained its 4.5-in gun on the attackers, but this also malfunctioned after firing just eight rounds. Closer in, HMS *Brilliant* locked on to one of the Skyhawks with her Sea Wolf system, designed as a final line of defence against low-flying aircraft and sea-skimming missiles, and which had never been used in anger before. The frigate quickly fired three Sea Wolf missiles: the first scored a direct hit on the A-4B flown by TT Nivoli, causing it to crash into the water. The second blew up the Skyhawk flown by TT Ibarlucea who had meanwhile released his bomb – which missed. While overflying *Brilliant*, Bustos saw another missile fired at him: while breaking to avoid, his aircraft hit the water and crashed. Vázquez managed to drop his bomb on HMS *Glasgow* and escaped unharmed at very low altitude. By the time he returned to Río Gallegos, his windscreen was covered with a salt crust to a degree where he could not see the runway: he veered off on landing, but without damaging the aircraft [4]

The second wave of this airstrike consisted of Oro Flight, which launched from Río Gallegos at 12:30 along the OF.1180. The formation included Capitán Antonio Zelaya (C-225), TT Juan Arrarás (C-244), PT Fausto Gavazzi (C-248) and Alférez Guillermo Dellepiane (C-239). Zelaya recalled:

Half an hour before the end of my duty, two fragmentary

orders arrived. The flight to the war zone was without problems. My navigation equipment went out of service and I had to make my navigation by time and heading. I continued leading the escadrille despite of this. The main problem I had was that the command changed the attack time by fifteen minutes, something hard to achieve on a flight launched on as short a note as ours. We arrived at the target seven minutes after what was expected from us [14:00]. We began the descent on the planned point, so we reached the sea level before Gran Malvina [West Falkland], which was Waypoint One of our navigation. Waypoint Two was Fitzroy settlement. Going to Waypoint Two I diverted slightly from my course, I guess this was by the tendency to fly following the coast and continuously watching the sky trying to avoid bad surprises. Halfway from waypoints One to Two I saw to my right Goose Green town, which should actually have been about seven miles to my left – if I would have followed the planned route. Thus, I corrected the course on reaching Waypoint Two, and then began our final approach to the target.

At Fitzroy I controlled my position and followed to the target. We flew in total radio silence. To both sides, wingmen Arrarás and Gavazzi were flying lower than me, which was logical, as I had to fly higher to control my navigation charts. We passed over the coast and continued east, descending a little bit more while I was searching for a target. This was supposed to be 25 kilometres

HMS *Glasgow* as seen on 12 May 1982, shortly before the attack.

A dramatic photograph showing the A-4B flown by PT Fausto Gavazzi just miliseconds away HMS *Glasgow* on 12 May. One of his bombs holed the destroyer, rendering it unserviceable, but in turn Gavazzi was shot down by friendly anti-aircraft artillery at Goose Green while attempting to return to the base.

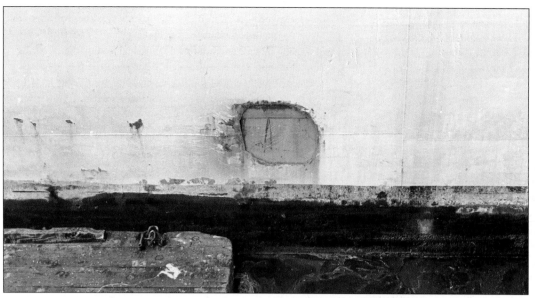

The patched bomb hole low on the starboard side of HMS *Glasgow*.

An A-4C Skyhawk of IV Brigada Aérea's Escuadrón I Aeromóvil, armed with three BR.250 bombs mounted on a TER under the centreline, takes off for another mission. Notable is the application of azure blue identification markings on the fin and the undersides of both drop tanks – a direct result of the downing of Gavazzi's A-4C by friendly anti-aircraft artillery on 12 May 1982.

it was a bomb, but then I left behind that idea, as we rapidly flew away: I did not stay to find out what it was, because when I saw my radio altimeter I thought I was too high and descended again. We started to return, while I was hearing my wingmen shouting happily. Then we evaluated the result of our attack. Arrarás said he believed he hit his ship, Gavazzi was completely sure and I had doubts, because I aimed to the stern and the speed of the ship surprised me. Dellepiane made the same aiming as me and he saw a helicopter on the flight deck of one of them.

Once we finished the checks we returned in pairs. Some minutes after leaving the target and flying over land, close to Goose Green, Wingman Four informed that Three had lost an aileron: seconds later, the aircraft turned upside down and crashed into the ground. Over Gran Malvina we were the three together. There Dellepiane had to climb fast to 40,000 feet because he had minimum fuel. With TT Arrarás we followed our low flight for 90 kilometres more and then we began to climb towards home. Nobody talked. On the final approach we realised we had the windscreens completely covered with salt, impeding the vision ahead. We tried to remove it, changing the hot air to cold air of the heating, but we couldn't. Arrarás had a very big bullet in one of his wings.

from the coast. We were travelling at 150 metres per second and I had planned to fly three minutes at that speed and heading: if we couldn't find our target by then, we would return. Eventually, I saw two ships in front of me: I think they were heading in south-southeastern direction, very fast, because I could see the spray from their bow. Our formation split: the front section heading for the ship to the north, and the other two for the one to the south, which was closer to my sight. Because of this decision, finally three aircraft attacked the ship sailing ahead and one the one behind her, because I also attacked the ship closest to me. Some kilometres before reaching the target, they opened fire. I didn't see missiles, but I heard the noise of the explosions of the AA fire [a 40mm Bofors gun on *Brilliant* and a 20mm Oerlikon on *Glasgow*, also a lot of light weapons from both ships, author's note]. At the moment I attacked I only watched the sight and the target. I didn't see the crew or helicopters, the only thing I remembered was the big radar antenna turning constantly.

After passing over the ships, my wingmen said the sea seemed to be boiling because of the bullets falling on the surface. I found myself at 1,000 feet and turning towards the ships to see what was happening. On the ship ahead there was a lot of movement and circles on the water, as if something fell into the sea. First I thought

Dellepiane was the newest pilot of the unit and – officially – still lacking all the necessary qualifications. For example, he had never trained for in-flight refuelling. He recalled:

Two flights were ordered to go with 5 minutes of difference between one and another. We carried thousand-pound bombs. I had never done air refuelling and many times people failed in the practices. This made me nervous: what a shame if I had to go back because I cannot refuel. It drove Gavazzi crazy, who was my boss, until one day he told me that I was going to do it well, that I was the first in the aviator course, the first also in the fighters' school.

We prepared our mission, the first flight took off, then we followed. We did the refuelling without problems, and we did our navigation, despite the haze. Close to the target, we learned that the first flight lost three aircraft shot down, but we continued until seeing the ships that were firing. They caused plenty of splashes in the sea.

We attacked, dropped our bombs, went out, each one in a different direction. I lost the visual contact to other members of the flight, but I set the course along which I planned to escape. Then I saw an A-4 ahead and it turned out to be Gavazzi. I approached and we returned together. The surprise was when Gavazzi, 10 minutes into the flight, was shot down and I was alone, he was hit on a wing, we were very low, he did not have time to eject. I ejected my tanks, I went lower and I remained half lost, because Gavazzi was guiding me. I was a little shocked until Zelaya reassured me. We continued the navigation, nothing was seen because of the conditions of the sea, the haze had formed a thick layer of salt crust on my windshield (the result of this experience was a study run by a biochemist, who had discovered that by spraying a thin layer of silicone over the windshield prevented this from happening again).

Once away from the islands, I started to climb, still flying all alone. Underway back home, we learned that [the] sole survivor of the first flight was Vazquez: he could not see anything and veered off the runway on landing. Us three managed to land: there was always an officer in the tower – in that case this was Cervera – and he directed us. We left with eight aircraft and returned with four. We could not identify what ship it was we attacked: we went in, we bombed it, and then the intelligence reported the ship name.

At the moment of this second attack, the defensive systems of HMS *Glasgow* were still out of action; HMS *Brilliant*'s Sea Wolf system malfunctioned too, and thus failed to fire. Thus, according to British sources, Gavazzi scored a direct hit, but his heavy bomb crashed all the way through *Glasgow* before detonating in the sea on the other side. Although the holes were covered and the ship could still sail, the damage caused led to the decision to send her back home on 27 May. HMS *Brilliant* only received minor damage from 20mm shells fired by Arrarás: his bomb ricocheted off the sea surface, bounced and passed over the ship. Gavazzi was then shot down by the FAA's own anti-aircraft artillery while passing BAM Cóndor. Overall, in its first

Table 7: A-4Cs of the Grupo 4 deployed at BAM Río Gallegos, 24 May 1982	
Version	Serial
A-4C	C-301
A-4C	C-302
A-4C	C-304
A-4C	C-305
A-4C	C-309
A-4C	C-310
A-4C	C-318
A-4C	C-319
A-4C	C-321
A-4C	C-322
A-4C	C-325

combat mission of the war, Grupo 5 de Casa Bombardeo lost four Skyhawks while damaging a destroyer of the Royal Navy.

The A-4C pilots from Escuadrón I Aeromóvil were less lucky: eight of them prepared for a mission in which every aircraft was to be armed with a single Mk.17, and the formation was to operate in cooperation with four Daggers armed with two BRP.500s each. However, the withdrawal of the British warships from the coast lead to the cancellation of this operation.

No further combat sorties were launched by either of the A-4 units for more than a week afterwards, even though training sorties were continued. Moreover, there was a constant requirement to replace aircraft in need of maintenance: correspondingly, on 15 May 1982, A-4C C-301 was sent to San Julián and on 20 May serial numbers C-305 and C-321 arrived, replacing C-319 and 322 sent to Mendoza for maintenance. The latter two returned on 24 May.

6
BOMB ALLEY

Late in the afternoon of 20 May 1982, a group of 16 amphibious assault ships, support ships and escorting warships detached from the Royal Navy's task force and turned west. The vessels carried the troops of 40 Commando and 45 Commando Royal Marines, and the 2nd and 3rd Battalions of the Parachute Regiment (2 Para and 3 Para) of the British Army, eighteen 105mm guns of 29 Commando Regiment Royal Artillery, the Commando Logistics Regiment, 59 Independent Commando Squadron Royal Engineers, the light helicopters of the Commando Brigade Air Squadron and 656 Squadron Army Air Corps, a troop of Rapier SAMs of T Battery 12 Air Defence Regiment Royal Artillery, and several support units. These were embarked on amphibious assault ships HMS *Fearless* (L10) and HMS *Intrepid* (L11), Landing Ship Logistics RFA *Sir Galahad* (L3005), RFA *Sir Lancelot* (L3029), RFA *Sir Tristram* (L3505), and RFA *Sir Percival* (L3036), and the roll-on/roll-off ferries MV *Norland* and MV *Europic Ferry*. They were escorted by the destroyer HMS *Antrim* (D18), frigates HMS *Broadsword* (F88), HMS *Brilliant* (F90), HMS *Plymouth* (F101), HMS *Argonaut* (F56), and HMS *Ardent* (F184), and RFA *Fort Austin* (A386). Circumnavigating north of the islands, the convoy moved relatively

slowly until reaching the northern entry to Falkland Sound/San Carlos Straight around 16:00, when helicopters deployed the Marines of the Special Boats Squadron and a Naval Gunfire Forward Observation officer on Fanning Head to attack an Argentine unit deployed there. Although run in rapidly improving weather and a rising new moon, thanks to a series of diversionary attacks elsewhere, these flights and the following passage of the entire convoy into Falkland Sound/San Carlos Strait all went unnoticed by the Argentines. It was only around dawn of 21 May 1982 that the Argentine Army units deployed in Port San Carlos realised that 'something was going on': by then, the British had secured their initial beachhead, had their amphibious assault and support ships anchored inside San Carlos Bay, and escorting warships in position within Falkland Sound/San Carlos Straight.

Of course, CdoFAS then received an entire stream of related reports: however, it took time for Brigadier-General Crespo to ascertain their reliability. Once he and his staff were sure that the British had actually landed, Crespo ordered almost all of his aircraft into action – even though with only minimal targeting intelligence: essentially, his pilots were advised to attack whatever ships they could find. Moreover, the

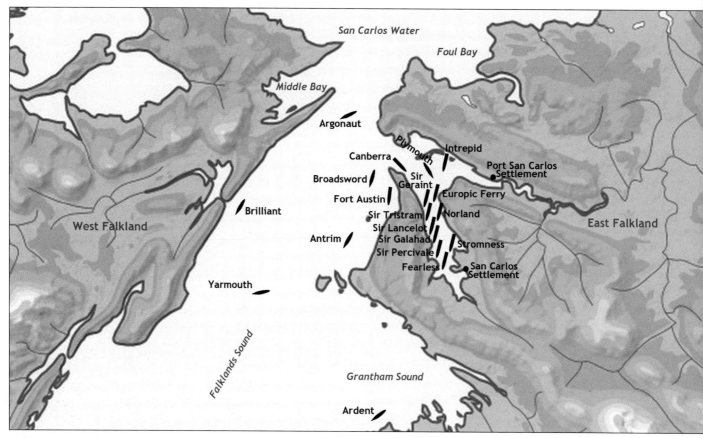

Approximate dispositions of the Royal Navy's warships and assault transports in Falkland Sound and San Carlos Bay, around 09:00 of 21 May 1982. (Diagram by Tom Cooper)

fighter-bombers involved received rather luke-warm support from four Mirage IIIEA interceptors: the crews of these failed to establish contact with the FAA's AN/TPS-43 radar and thus failed to distract any of the Royal Navy's Sea Harriers that flew combat air patrols west and south of Falkland Sound/San Carlos Straight.

Interception by Sea Harriers

The first Skyhawks to launch were A-4Cs of Escuadrón I Aeromóvil: operational order OF.1187 scrambled Tero Flight from San Julián at 11:17. The formation included TT Néstor López (C-309) and TT Castillo (C-314). However, because the wingman had to abort, López then joined the next flight, Pato (OF.1188), including Capitán Eduardo Almoño (C-310), Alférez Guillermo Martínez (C-302) and PT Daniel Manzotti (C-325), which took off at 11:25. All aircraft were armed with one Mk.17 bomb. Minutes after them, Rondó Flight was launched under OF.1191, including Capitán Jorge Garía (C-304) and Alférez Gerardo Isaac. However, Isaac was forced to abort due to engine-related problems, and García thus also joined Pato Flight, which grew to six aircraft. The formation left the KC-130H at 12:54 and turned towards West Falkland/Gran Malvina but was detected early by the radar of HMS Brilliant. The frigate promptly vectored a pair of Sea Harriers – flown by Lieutenant-Commander Mike Blisset (in XZ496) and Lieutenant-Commander Neil Thomas (in XZ492) – to intercept. The Royal Navy pilots caught the Skyhawks over the area of Chartress Settlement and Blisset promptly shot down Manzotti's jet with a single AIM-9L. The pilot was killed. Seconds later, Thomas's missile hit López's aircraft, causing it to crash. The rest of the formation jettisoned their bombs and escaped west.

The first A-4Bs to go were four aircraft of Mula Flight, launched at 11:30 under OF.1189. These included Capitán Carballo (C-204), TT Rinke (C-231), PT Cachón (C-250) and Alférez Carmona (C-214). Cachón aborted with technical problems and the others continued to

the islands arriving over Queen Charlotte Bay/San Julián. Over West Falkland /Gran Malvina, Rinke's Skyhawk suffered a failure of the fuel system, forcing the pilot to abort. The remaining two A-4Bs diverted slightly to the south, because the Hornsby Mountains were covered by clouds. Carballo recalled:

When we were flying along the west side of the Hornsby Mountains, I turned to the east. I saw my wingman close, searching for San Carlos Strait/Falkland Sound, I jumped the cliff and put my aircraft as low as I could, very close to the sea. Alférez Carmona said 'to the right'. In a bay to the other side of the Sound I saw a big ship and began my attack. While approaching I saw it wasn't a warship, it was big and white and fearing it was one of ours I didn't fire, asking Carmona to also stop attacking, but I heard him saying 'I released!'

Although the pilots were informed that they had attacked a British amphibious ship, there are no records of one of the Royal Navy's vessels being subject to such an attack in this area. However, the ELMA Río Carcarañá was within King Harbour, a few kilometres further southwest and slightly to the right of the ingress route of Mula Flight. Although the FAA denies this attack hit the abandoned vessel, all the known details indicate that Carmona struck it with his bomb.

While ordering his wingman to return, Carballo continued along the eastern side of the sound until reaching Grantham Sound/Ruiz Puente, where he found HMS Ardent in the process of shelling Argentine Army positions in the Goose Green area. Carballo promptly attacked, firing his 20mm cannons while approaching: he released his bomb and then passed so low over the Royal Navy warship that he had to bank his aircraft to avoid hitting one of the ship's masts. On the way out, he passed by the destroyer HMS Antrim – which failed to open fire at the low-flying Skyhawk – and was then tracked by HMS Brilliant, the crew of which directed a pair of Sea Harriers flown by

Lieutenant-Commanders Neil Thomas and Mike Blissett to intercept. However, the British failed to find the Argentine flight-leader, and Carballo thus returned to his base safely.

Attack on HMS *Argonaut*

The next to become airborne – shortly after 11:30, operating under OF.1190 – was Pico Flight of Escuadrón II Aeromóvil, including Capitán Palaver (C-207), TT Daniel Gálvez (C-221), PT Guadagnini (C-212) and Alférez Gómez (C-226). After one fighter-bomber was forced to abort due to technical problems, this formation reached San Carlos, but found no targets.

HMS *Argonaut* seen from a nearby ship, shortly after the frigate was hit.

The order OF.1196 scrambled Orión and Leo flights at 12:30. The first included PT Velasco (C-225), and TTs Carlos Ossés (C-239) and Fernando Robledo (C-222), and the second PT Alberto Filippini (C-215), Alférez Rubén Vottero (C-224) and TT Vicente Autiero (C-240). The aircraft were armed with one Mk.17 bomb each. Filippini recalled:

> The leader of the first flight aborted due to a technical failure, so I took charge of all aircraft. In turn, I lost control over my wingman, about whom I heard only after the landing. Because of the particular characteristics of the islands, with a lot of bays and small rivers, we made our navigation by time. It was also very difficult because of the rain, fog and wind. We arrived at our acceleration point three minutes before reaching the target zone, and while underway at a mere 10ft altitude (3.3 metres)!
>
> When I saw San Carlos, one of my wingmen called, "To the Right!" I considered this an order, banked and turned in that direction to find a frigate underway in the north of the Sound. The frigate saw us too, and was sailing towards a very high cliff, to force us to climb. Next, we began to receive enemy anti-aircraft fire: there were explosions ahead of us, and some above us, all forcing us to descend even more. We moved into the blind zone of the frigate's guns, then turned and began to aim our bombs. I concentrated on aiming, dropped my bomb, then pulled on the stick to climb while turning to the right, to avoid that cliff. Then I felt a very strong knock underneath the aircraft: I had hit one of [the] ship's antennas with one of my drop tanks, breaking its tail cone. On the way out, I saw another frigate in front of me [probably HMS *Broadsword*; author's note]. I made a max-g turn to the left, calling my wingmen to follow me. Then I saw an explosion on the land nearby: probably a missile fired by the ship I was trying to avoid. Finally, I descended low between the mountains to hide. We followed a valley until reaching the sea north of Isla Soledad (East Falkland), and then continued at very low altitude until passing the northern entry into the Sound. While underway there, we saw the frigate we had attacked exploding.

Indeed, the flights led by Filippini left the frigate HMS *Argonaut* hit by two bombs: while both failed to detonate, they damaged the engines and the ruder, they caused two Sea Cat short-range SAMs to explode, and created several holes that caused flooding. While remaining in

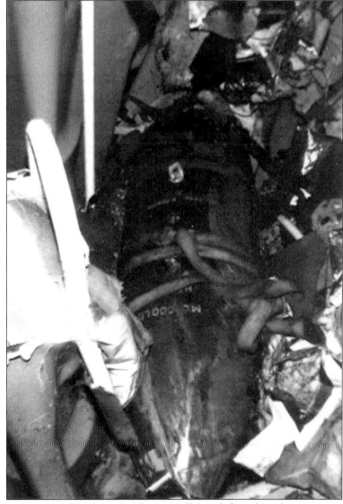
A British made Mk.17 1000lb bomb found inside HMS *Argonaut*, where it was deposited by the A-4Bs of Escuadrón II Aeromóvil on 21 May 1982.

the San Carlos area until most urgent repairs were carried out, and – although using her radar to detect incoming airstrikes – the ship was actually out of the fight: on 3 June, HMS *Argonaut* was sent back to the United Kingdom.

On the contrary, the A-4Cs took no part in the third wave, but only in the fourth – and final – wave of the day. Following OF.1201,

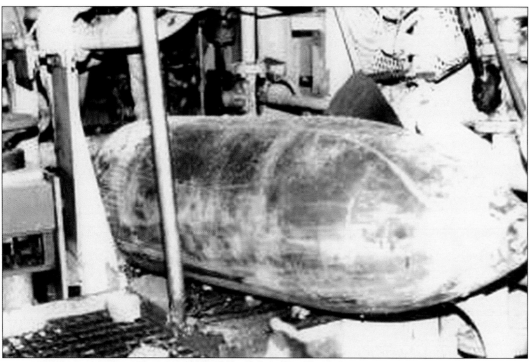

The second Mk.17 bomb found inside HMS *Argonaut*.

HMS *Argonaut* on her return to England.

I flew my first mission on 21 May to relieve Escuadrón 1 Aeromóvil, as they had engaged with all of their aircraft and my unit was on readiness. We launched at sunset and arrived when the islands were already covered in darkness. We did look for targets but could not find any.

3° Escuadrilla's First Combat Mission: Strike on HMS *Ardent*

Operating on its own, COAN's 3° Escuadrilla saw its first combat operations on 21 May 1982. The first flight – including CC Castro Fox (3-A-301), TC Medici (3-A-307), TN Benitez (3-A-312), CC Zubizarreta (3-A-306), TN Olmedo (3-A-304), and TN Oliveira (3-A-305) – launched at 10:10. Because the Omega nav/attack systems on both 3-A-301 and 3-A-306 (the only ones equipped with it) failed, navigation proved extremely problematic. Fox and his wingmen spent 15 minutes searching for targets before deciding to return to their base. A new attack mission was ordered for the same afternoon.

With both Omega navigational systems remaining unserviceable, Castro Fox decided to operate in two flights of three aircraft instead, still all armed with four Mk.82 bombs each (plus 200 rounds for their two 20mm cannons). The first to go was the flight including CC Alberto Philippi (3-A-307), TF Marquez (3-A-314) and TN José César Arca (3-A-312). This launched at 14:10. Philippi recalled:

The parameters to attack were an approach at very low altitude, 50ft, at the speed of 450 knots, to avoid radar detection until the last moment. Close to the ship to be attacked, about 1,500 meters, we had to stop evasive manoeuvres and climb to 300 feet and then fly straight to fire guns and to wait until our pipper sight would pass through the target before pressing the button to release bombs. When you drop four Mk.82 bombs from an aircraft as light as the A-4Q, the aircraft 'jumps' up: we had to keep this in mind before pushing the throttle lever to full power and starting evasive manoeuvres to escape and avoid being followed by the fire control radars or the missiles from the ships.

The second flight took off 15 minutes later. It consisted of TN Benito Rótolo (3-A-306), TN Lecour (3-A-305) and TN Sylvester (3A-301). Philippi continued:

Raspón Flight launched at 15:45, including Capitán Mario Caffarati (on C-305) and TT Ricardo Lucero (C-310), while the third aircraft aborted. Fifteen minutes later, Choclo Flight took off under OF.1202, including Capitán Jorge Pierini (C-318), PT Ernesto Ureta (C-304), and TT Daniel Méndez (on C-301). All aircraft were armed with Mk.17s. The two flights reached the target zone undisturbed but, after circling for several minutes, found nothing worth their attention and returned to their base at 17:45 and 18:00, respectively.

The last mission launched by Escuadrón II Aeromóvil on 21 May 1982 was undertaken under CdoFAS order OF.1203, as part of the fourth wave. Mate Flight included A-4Bs flown by Captain Carlos Varela (C-207), Lieutenants Mario Roca (C-214) and Sergio Mayor (C-242) and Alférez Marcelo Moroni (C-212), all armed with Mk.17 bombs, which took-off at 16:30 and joined two flights of A-4Cs.

Reaching the combat zone at sunset, the pilots found the visibility was so poor that they could not find any targets. Thus, they returned to base at 19:00. Moroni recalled:

We climbed to 27,000ft and joined our formation. The distance to the target was 385 nautical miles [620km; author's note]. We began to descend as trained before the war, 100 miles short of the target, and then flew the last 50 miles at an altitude of 100ft over the sea surface. The time to target was 58 minutes. I didn't have a navigation computer or VLF Omega, so I navigated using the magnetic compass and the ADF signal until I started the descent.

Once at very low altitude, navigation was calculated by heading, speed, time – i.e. with compass and watch – and visual references, if there were any. The islands appeared to my sight, covered by the clouds, about five minutes earlier than expected, which showed me we had more tailwind than announced. We made a more pronounced descent, because we were closer, and the British could have detected us. Then as we reached the Isla Pájaro [Bird Island; author's note] we pushed our master arm [switch] on, continued to the southwest of Gran Malvina, and then turned right, flying along the coast all the way to Belgrano [Cape Meredith; author's note]. The cloud base was at about 500ft, but we remained well below it, flying through showers that cut the visibility down to less than one mile: this forced my wingmen to tighten the formation in order to retain visual contact. When we reached Belgrano, I turned left to cross the southern entry into Falkland Sound/San Carlos Strait, to a heading of 070 degrees. The cape in front was black and threatening as a bad omen, its top covered by a cloud. The visibility suddenly reduced – so much so there was a Royal Navy frigate that detected us from a distance of 15 miles, and then fired missiles from 5 miles. We could not see that ship before we were around 4 miles away – and had no radar warning receivers to at least know we have been painted by the enemy radar.

I kept my course, leading the flight as planned. Crossing the southern end of the sound and still not detecting any ships, I continued north-east while searching for the secondary target – one of the ships in San Carlos Bay. Reaching the coast of Isla Soledad [East Falkland; author's note], I turned to heading 025° and flew 50ft low over the beach at 450 knots, while my wingmen spread into attack formation: I was in front, with Márquez behind and Arca to my right. The weather began improving fast as we approached: just before reaching Bahia de Ruiz Puente [Grantham Sound/Ruiz Puente; author's note] we saw masts and antennas of a ship about five miles ahead of us, appearing behind North West Island, in the north. I called my wingmen to make them aware that this is our target and gave the order to attack. My first intention was to approach directly, using the protection of the rock in front of us. However, I had to change the attack route due to the surprising speed of the ship: appearing from behind the rock, this began to move towards the centre of the Sound. It was shortly before 15:00, and I was watching the movement of the ship: I assumed they had detected us, so I turned to the right, and then smoothly to the left, trying to hide my aircraft form the radar against the backdrop of the coast. When I assumed I was at the right distance, I broke left and thus reached the best position to attack from the port side of the ship, along the heading of 250 degrees. Arca, who was meanwhile to my left, remained inside my turn and thus couldn't keep his position: he went to the right, remaining my Number 2. The frigate was now roughly on the heading of 225°, sailing at maximum speed, before it turned left as we approached. When in gun range, I pressed the trigger, but both guns jammed after firing only a few shots.

The frigate was HMS *Ardent* (F184), a ship involved in the bombardment of Argentine positions at Goose Green. Arca recalled:

At the start of our attack run, I was too close to Philippi's aircraft: only some 7-10 seconds, instead of the required 19. I didn't try to correct this because there was no time nor space: the British opened heavy anti-aircraft fire, causing plenty of splashes in the water, and explosions very close to my aircraft. I recall that during the approach I saw a missile leaving the ship: I broke hard to the right to avoid, and then returned to my original course. Because I was so close behind the leader, we released our bombs almost simultaneously: still, I could see Philippi's bombs falling down, their tails opening and establishing the desired separation between them. Until then I had hopes that he could miss so that his bombs would be no problem for me, but it was not like this: the fourth bomb hit the stern causing a Dantesque explosion, and I had no chance of evading, I flew straight through a thick ball of flames and smoke as I was releasing my bombs and called the leader to inform him, "one on the stern". Then I heard Márquez, "another one on the stern".

We turned away and flew down the coast from where we came. I saw my leader to my left, about 1,000 metres ahead of me, and about 1,000-1,500 metres away and to the right was Márquez. A mere 15 seconds later, he said, "there are Sea Harriers". I looked at the leader and saw a Sidewinder missile being fired and then flying into his exhaust nozzle. I looked to my right and I didn't see Márquez but another Sea Harrier and almost simultaneously my aircraft was hit by the first burst of 30mm into the right wing. I was flying at no more than 10ft over the water, and the hit almost caused me to crash. I managed to control my aircraft and tried to search for the one who shot at me, so he couldn't hit me again, but then I received another hit: I lost all the hydraulic pressure, the oxygen supply, and a part of electrical power, and thus prepared to eject. At 480 knots I changed to manual control, despite the hardening of the commands, as the NATOPS manual [Naval Air Training and Operating Procedures Standardization; author's note] indicated a maximum of 250 knots to do this. I tried to turn to face one of the Sea Harriers. The combat lasted for about 40 seconds but they left me, I don't know why. Maybe they were short on fuel or had no ammunition. I headed for Puerto Argentino following the coast, trying to avoid Goose Green, flying very low at 500 knots and with manual controls, looking for the fuel indicator, 100 pounds and decreasing, because of the holes I had in the wings, six on the left and four on the right one. My next preoccupation was to avoid hitting the ground because of the conditions in which I was flying and also to inform the defences at Puerto Argentino about my approach to avoid being fired on.

After a lot of calls, I contacted a helicopter from the Army, and asked them to act as radio relay to the ground control. Approaching the runway, I lowered the landing gear and the indicator showed the nose wheel and the right main wheel safe, but the left one was not secured. I told this to the controller and asked him for permission to fly over the tower so they can verify this. He said "look, the left landing gear disappeared, there's only the hole and I can see the sky through the holes you have in your plane, go and eject over the bay". I had no choice, my intention was to land the aircraft and save it. I climbed to 2,500 feet and went to the ejection point. I took off my mask, which I had buckled only on one side and then ejected using the upper handle. It's a very hard moment, as you don't know what will happen after, and still, you do all of that automatically.

After the violent explosion and feeling the sensation of doing stunts in my seat during the exit, I found myself hanging from my parachute and surrounded by a total silence. The aircraft did not want to abandon me, as with a smooth turn and descending, it almost came back to hit me. The Skyhawk made two turns until, because of the danger it presented, the flak opened fire and shot it down. Meanwhile, I inflated my vest, took off my gloves and – due to the proximity to the water – I did not release the dinghy. Instead, I prepared to release the parachute as soon as I hit the water. Once in the water an Army UH-1H approached to start the rescue. As they were not prepared for this task, they didn't have a crane to hoist me. After some failed attempts for half an hour, surviving thanks to the immersion suit, the pilot put the skis into the water and I took hold of one with my hands and feet and we flew to the coast, about 500 meters, where I released the ski and the helicopter landed so I could get in, and then they took me to the hospital.

The Skyhawks of 3° Escuadrilla were attacked by Lieutenant Clive Morrell in Sea Harrier FRS.Mk 1 coded XZ457/14, and Fight-Lieutenant John Leeming in XZ500 (both from 800 Naval Air Squadron, embarked on HMS *Hermes*). Morrell first shot down Philippi with a Sidewinder and then attempted to engage Arca, but his second AIM-9L failed to launch: seconds later, the missile did fire, but then crashed into the sea. Morrell thus opened fire with his 30mm cannon. Philippi ejected safely but was rescued only days later. Leeming first fired a burst at Márquez's A-4Q but missed: then he fired again and the Skyhawk exploded, killing its unlucky pilot. The action was still not over, however: only minutes later, the second flight arrived on the scene. Sylvester commented:

Our mission was to attack a damaged ship in the southern end of Falkland Sound [possibly ELMA *Río Carcarañá*, sought by Air Force aircraft and mistakenly identified as a British ship; author's note] and if we could not find it, continue to San Carlos to attack the first enemy ship we could see. The navigation went well and we arrived at the expected place. We turned to the right and went to Águila/Speedwell Island to look for the damaged ship. We heard

the communication of the leader of the first escadrille saying he was ejecting and immediately I tried to communicate with the others, but I received no reply. We tightened the formation and we continued flying in a column, so we could follow the leader, and we ended in Grantham Sound/Ruiz Puente. We saw four ships and the leader told us to attack the closest one, so we started the attack pattern at low altitude and high speed.

Benito Rótolo continued:

When this mission was ordered, the A-4Qs were refuelled and armed to depart at about 14:00, having to be quick because of the few hours of daylight. When we made the briefing of the mission, we were informed that there was a target that was probably a damaged transport in the southern part of Falkland Sound/San Carlos Strait. The idea was to reach the target, bomb it and try to sink it: if we found any other targets, we were to do the same. Minutes after that, while we were putting our flying suits on, the command informed us that the ship wasn't alone and maybe had two or three escorts. Later, while we were inspecting the aircraft before our departure, new information arrived: there was no transport, but we were to expect a lot of units of the Royal Navy supporting the landing of their ground troops. Our mission now was to attack the first ship we could find inside the operational zone.

Originally, an S-3E Tracker was to fly reconnaissance of the southern side of Falkland Sound/San Carlos Strait, but we did not have the time to organise in-flight refuelling and were to operate at the limit of our range. Thus, the mission was launched because there was urgency to attack as soon as possible. The take-off was normal, despite the condition of the runway of Río Grande. It was better than to do it on an aircraft carrier, but anyway it was marginal. Everything worked normally; we flew separated 10 minutes from

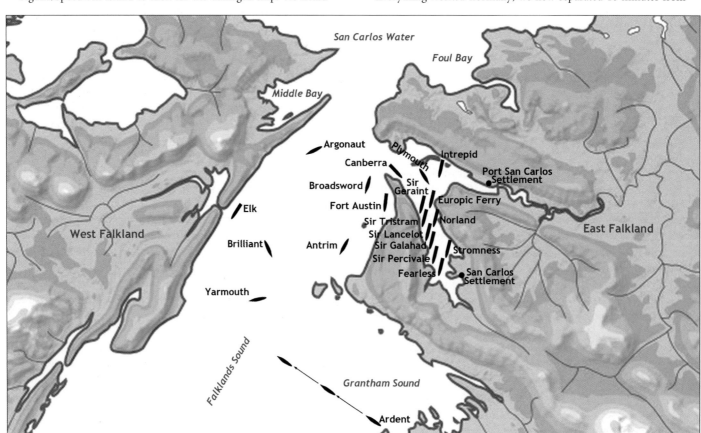

Approximate dispositions of Royal Navy warships and assault transports during the afternoon of 21 May, when the frigate HMS *Ardent* was subjected to successive airstrikes by FAA Daggers and COAN A-4s. (Diagram by Tom Cooper)

the other three aircraft. We couldn't accelerate too much to reach them because we had to take care of the fuel: our reserve was minimal, and we had to keep in mind the option of being damaged and losing fuel. Because of this it wasn't easy to think about a safe return.

Because the Tracker operated from a different aerodrome than ours and because of a misunderstanding, we didn't coincide on the moment to reach the target and we didn't have contact with the S-3E before the attack. When we were close to the start the descent, at 100 miles from the islands, flying at 30,000 feet, we heard some communications of the other group, that were inside the strait at that time. The information they gave us was that the small islands we saw on the charts were very low, so we couldn't hide behind them to prevent us from being detected by the enemy radars. Also, they told us that the ship

A-4Qs of 3° Escuadrilla at Río Grande on 20 May 1982, together with three Learjets of the Air Force, one B-200 and two Fokker F.28s of the Navy. Among the Skyhawks is 3-A-307, shot down on the following day.

HMS *Ardent* afire and listing before sinking.

that was to be in the southern part of Falkland Sound/San Carlos Strait wasn't there.

We began to descend when we heard Teniente Márquez saying that he had found a destroyer in the middle of the strait. Captain Philippi said: "attack her". They attacked the ship, we heard nothing more, until finally we heard Márquez saying "Harrier, Harrier" and later a voice that I believe was of Capitán Philippi saying: "I'm ejecting". This is how we realised that the Sea Harriers were there too.

There were other options, but we decided to complete our mission, though with the difference that we would cross the southern part of the strait and continue over East Falkland to avoid detection. I asked my wingmen if they were with me to do the mission and they answered yes.

Finally we arrived over Grantham Sound/Ruiz Puente and turned to cross. At that moment we saw some ships, one in the centre of the sound, looking like a Type 21 Frigate. We turned and attacked right away: there was no time for finding a better route, and when loaded with 2,000 pounds of bombs and all the fuel, at the speed of 450 knots, the Skyhawk has a turn radius of four miles.

As we approached the target, we realised there were other ships, obscured by the shadows of the coast, squalls, and rain. A few were more visible because they were out in the sun. They opened fire at us as we approached perpendicular to our target, followed by the Type 21 Frigate in front of us: this fired her machine guns. There were lots of impacts on the water, to which we reacted with the classic zig-zag turns to shake off the aim of enemy gunners. This was not particularly effective, but it was the only thing we could do. Through our attack, while flying close to the water, we did not separate by 20 seconds between single aircraft, but all went in

together. Shortly before releasing, I climbed to 200ft, to enable the fuses to arm the bombs following release. This seemed too high to me, so after dropping my bombs, I rolled the aircraft inverted to descend faster: this was something normal at 10,000ft, but in this case I rolled out only a few feet above the water surface!

Then I made a tight turn to the left so to return to the south inside the channel, but I found a County-class destroyer in front of me [HMS *Antrim*, D18; author's note], and she opened fire with all of her weapons. I ordered my wingmen "turn again over my axis, to the right": I looked back and saw Sylvester and Lecour releasing their bombs, some of which I could actually see. They got the message and we all escaped flying very low, almost touching the water, until we reached the first hill on the coast. There we climbed over and behind it. While we were flying across some valleys I asked my wingmen if they could inspect each other's aircraft: Lecour was following me very close, but Sylvester was separated far behind. At that moment we heard the voice of the Tracker pilot informing us that he was ready to guide us, thinking that we were just arriving in the operations zone…

The attack was very effective, we couldn't talk because the enemy could find our position, and the worst part was to come. To escape we were obligated to climb fast to reduce the fuel consumption and we feared that we were still inside the range of the Sea Dart SAMs of the Type 42 Destroyers. Eventually, there was no other option: we climbed up to 28,000-29,000ft on passing the western-most part of the archipelago, then continued all the way up to 40,000ft, which was the upper ceiling of the Sea Dart. Without talking, only with hand signals we then re-grouped.

It was a very hard moment because we became conscious of what we had done: only five minutes lapsed since we turned to attack that

The remains of A-4Q 3-A-312 after the ejection of TN Julio César Arca outside Puerto Argentino on 21 May 1982.

ship in the centre of the sound and until the time we started to climb. Three of these were under very high tension, being shot at, and flying much closer to the water surface than during exercises. With the exception of the separation between the aircraft, we had the additional ingredient of the psychological effect as a result of being under fire.

When we were at about 150 miles from Río Grande we informed the base about our return, and asked about the other flight. They answered that they never returned. Calculating the time passed they don't have enough fuel, so we confirmed they were shot down.

About our attack: Lecour and Sylvester, who was the last on the bombing run, saw that of my bombs two passed over the ship and two were short. Lecour, with his bombs had left the frigate surrounded by smoke and fire. This forced Sylvester to drop his bombs while he was crossing the smoke column produced by the bombs.

Finally, we arrived at Río Grande with so little fuel that we couldn't fly the usual circuit around the airport. Once on the ground, we realised this was our baptism of fire: we lost three pilots and three aircraft, and Sylvester's and Lecour's jets were also damaged in a few places.

During a post-war meeting between Rótolo and Alan West, former skipper of HMS *Ardent*, the latter confirmed that his ship was first damaged by Daggers, and that then both of 3° Escuadrilla's flights scored additional hits: the first three aircraft hit with two bombs, destroying the Sea Cat SAM system and damaging the stern. The second section then hit with one bomb (released by Lecour), which detonated underneath the rear fuel tank. West was left with no choice but to beach his ship to buy time for the evacuation of the crew to HMS *Yarmouth*. As a consequence of the Argentine strike, 22 crewmembers were killed and HMS *Ardent* was lost.

The Bad Weather of 22 May

CdoFAS planned to launch another series of airstrikes against the beachhead of San Carlos on 22 May. However, bad weather caused the cancellation of all but a handful of these. Escuadrón I Aeromóvil planned a joint mission with 3° Escuadrilla of COAN. Correspondingly, the Navy's A-4Qs were to attack the British troops in San Carlos Settlement, while Leon Flight (OF.1204) of A-4Cs was to hit the enemy ships in Sussex Bay. 3° Escuadrilla eventually cancelled both of its missions due to the bad weather. However, the A-4Cs of Leon Flight launched at 14:40, including Capitán Mario Caffarati (C-

304), TT Jorge Bono (C-314), PT Ernesto Ureta (C-310), and Alférez Carlos Codrington. However, because the pilots could not establish radio contact to the forward observer, and due the bad weather, the mission was aborted. On the way back, the formation saw a ship near the east coast of San Carlos but Caffarati decided not to attack because they were in a bad position to do so. This was just as well, because the ship in question was ELMA *Río Carcarañá*, disabled by Sea Harriers on 16 May, and abandoned by her crew. On the return, Ureta and Codrington had to refuel from KC-130H serial TC-70. By the end of the day the unit received a new reinforcement, with the arrival of A-4C serial C-324.

Another exception was Chispa Flight of Escuadrón II Aeromóvil, launched at 15:16 on order OF.1207, to bomb a ground target at Sussex Harbour with six A-4Bs, flown by Capitán Varela, PTs Héctor Sánchez and Oscar Berrier, and TTs Luis Cervera, Roca and Mayor. The last four jets all aborted due to technical failures, while the other two delivered their bombs on instruments-only because they could not see the ground below them. On their way out of the combat zone, the pilots suddenly saw two ships about 500 meters off the coast and then two Sea King helicopters. Héctor 'Pipi' Sánchez recalled:

We went as four aircraft to the air refuelling, first Varela and me, but he had problems and said he would return. When the other two went to the tanker, they also had problems and returned, so I said to them 'you can't leave me alone'. Varela returned and then he managed to refuel and we went in together. The weather was very bad. We arrived from the west over West Falkland/Gran Malvina to fly straight into lots of rain and low clouds. We were really scared, because we knew we only had a 50% chance to survive this mission. Following a mountain chain from north to south, I saw the mountains, the peaks of which were inside the clouds. We had no option but to climb: I checked my map and the height of the peaks, and was sure they could detect us with their radars. Thus we descended again as soon as we passed the mountains. I searched for Varela, then saw him flying diagonally from the south of Gran Malvina to San Carlos. My aircraft had no Omega (only a few aircraft had it), and thus I depended on him. Our target was on the ground, and we were carrying three BRPs each. When we arrived at San Carlos, I asked him, 'let me know when you drop the bombs!' and he replied, 'I just did so', so I dropped mine, too, immediately. We saw some tracers, but they were only firing with light guns. We arrived at the bay and when I was jumping the hills I saw a British helicopter and then two frigates. I continued flying alone, as I couldn't see the leader. Then we returned without problems.

23 May: The FAA Attack on HMS *Antelope*

On 23 May, the CdoFAS issued a new set of orders for attacks on ships in the San Carlos area: by this time, it was clear that the British beachhead was well-established, but the FAA wanted to make the process of unloading reinforcements and supplies as difficult as possible. Until then, the pilots were only instructed to 'attack ships', and thus usually went after the first vessel they could find – mostly heavily-armed destroyers and frigates providing protection for amphibious assault and support ships, underway in Falkland Sound/San Carlos Strait. Henceforth, they were advised to focus on the supply ships and landing vessels. Once again, the staff of the CdoFAS envisaged a multi-wave strike. The first consisted of a flight with six Daggers and two flights of three A-4Bs, the last all armed with one Mk.17 bomb each. OF.1207 launched Lanza Flight including PT Velasco (C-221), TT Fernando Robledo (C-215) and Alférez Jorge Barrionuevo (C-226). OF.1208 sent Tejo Flight into action with PT Filippini (C-214), Captain Jorge Bergamaschi (C-231) and TT Autiero (C-244). Both launched at 09:05, but the leader of the first and the Number 2 of the second formation had to abort for technical reasons. Ultimately, about 20 miles short of the target the two flights joined into a single formation: they reached San Carlos at 10:05 but could not find any targets and returned to Río Gallegos.

A-4B C-240 as seen from one of the KC-130H tankers. This aircraft was not only involved in attacks on HMS *Argonaut* and HMS *Antelope*, but also survived the war. The forward sections of the three BR.250 bombs mounted on a TER under the centreline are visible.

The second wave included two flights of A-4Bs: OF.1210 ordered Trueno into the air, including Captain Palaver, Alférez Gómez (C-240) and PT Guadagnini (C-242). However, the leader of the formation had problems starting his engine and thus his wingmen joined Nene Flight (OF.1211), composed of Capitán Carballo (C-228), with PTs Rinke (C-239) and Cachón. Moreover, Cachón slipped off the ladder while boarding his aircraft, and was injured. Thus, only four instead of six A-4Bs took off, each armed with one Mk.17. Arriving at the assigned refuelling point, the pilots realised that the KC-130H wasn't there, but 150 kilometres further north. Carballo recalled:

I asked the Hercules crewmembers where they were: to my surprise they said they were "over the rocks" – which meant over Grand Malvina. I asked them to head in our direction so we could find them on the way.

Finally, the two formations met, and the IFR-operation was concluded smoothly. The Skyhawks then pushed towards their objective, descending as they went. Flying very low, they passed Barren Island/Isla Pelada, then turned to a heading of 020 degrees, passed close to King Harbour where a smoke column was rising from the wreck of the abandoned ELMA *Río Carcarañá*, which had been attacked by a Westland Lynx helicopter from the frigate HMS *Antelope* (F170). Reaching Goose Green, Carballo decided to pass to the east of BAM Cóndor, to avoid the local anti-aircraft fire, and then turned west to pass over Grantham Sound/Ruiz Puente. Approaching San Carlos, the pilots next saw the Lynx helicopter from HMS *Antelope* returning from her attack, and thus turned to attack. Carballo's guns both jammed; Gómaz's only fired a few shots before doing the same, while the other two pilots could not fire because of the front pair of Skyhawks ahead of them. The formation pressed on and reached San Carlos Bay to find the frigates *Antelope* and *Broadsword* there, both of which promptly opened fire. Passing low over Fanning Head, the flight turned right, hidden by low hills north of the bay. Carballo continued:

I thought to perform the final attack from San Carlos Bay, but then I realised they will be waiting for us there, so I started a turn to my left over Verde Mountains, to the south of San Carlos Settlement, to attack the target from the north of the bay and heading west. Only Alférez Gómez followed me, as PT Guadagnini and TT Rinke lost me and began the attack from another direction. While we were approaching the frigates, the anti-aircraft fire was becoming more intense, so I descended to hide behind a small hill while approaching: this was a mistake that almost cost my life, because I was tracked by the radar of another frigate, which launched a missile which exploded below my left wing [in fact it was a Rapier missile launched from the coast; author's note]. I felt my aircraft was hit by the enemy fire. Later Alférez Gómez told me that a blue cloud covered my aircraft (apparently the blast) and a lot of rocks were raised from the ground: one of those hit one of my drop tanks, damaging the fin of it. He flew across the rocks, reaching the target and dropping his bomb. Immediately I thought 'I don't want to fall into the water', so I pulled my stick and returned over the Verde Mountains, while I informed the others of my decision to eject.

Meanwhile, the other pair was going towards a group of about nine ships in San Carlos Bay, one of which was very large and painted white – probably SS *Canberra* [in fact, this was the SS *Norland*; author's note].

Primer-Teniente Guadagnini started to turn so to attack his target from behind, the least-well defended area, while Rinke attacked directly, so he passed overhead first. Guadagnini's aircraft was hit in the wing, and he almost hit the water, but levelled again and hit the mast of HMS *Antelope*: his Skyhawk broke and exploded over the deck. While the ship was still moving after the impact of the aircraft, Guadagnini's bomb then hit the hull.

Meanwhile I realised I could still control my aircraft. This made me very happy, as the idea to eject wasn't attractive. Suddenly I saw a light to my right and turning my head I saw a missile launched from the ground, with orange, yellow and white lights, passing very close to my aircraft (this was a Sea Cat SAM launched from HMS *Antelope*; author's note). It was evident that because they fired too close they could not aim correctly.

The three remaining aircraft headed to the west on their way back, but Gómez's aircraft was badly damaged and he declared an emergency. Carballo all the time carefully controlled his instruments, preparing himself for a possible ejection because of the damage cause by the Rapier. Still over West Falkland/Gran Malvina, Carballo then saw the Embraer EMB.111 (serial 2-P-201) of the COAN, on a reconnaissance flight. Not recognizing the type – because this was still new in service and this was only the second operation sortie over the islands – the Argentine flight-leader decided to hold his fire. His formation landed at Río Gallegos at 15:30, followed by the very same EMB.111.

The downing of Guadagnini was subsequently claimed by HMS *Broadsword*'s Sea Wolf team (this fired two missiles), HMS *Antelope*'s gunners operating Oerlikon 20mm cannons, and the shore-based Rapier SAM team. HMS *Yarmouth*, HMS *Plymouth*, HMS *Argonaut*, HMS *Arrow* (F173), and HMS *Brilliant* (F90), were also nearby, and some of them opened fire, but none was attacked. The bomb released by Gómez actually missed *Broadsword* very narrowly; the one released by Rinke missed *Antelope*, but Guadagnini's bomb did score a hit – yet failed to detonate immediately. However, it did so the following night, when a bomb-disposal team was working on it. The detonation promptly caused a fire that spread, forcing HMS *Antelope*'s skipper to issue the dreadful order to abandon ship. Shortly before dawn, the fire reached the ammunition magazines, causing a massive explosion that broke the hull into two. By sunrise, only the tip of the bow and the stern were still afloat.

Escuadrón I Aeromóvil was also in action on 23 May 1982. Operating under OF.1212, Plata Flight – including Alférez Gerardo Isaac (C-305), PT Jorge Vázquez (C-324) and PT Omar Castillo (C-319) – took off at 11:30. Together with them went Oro Flight (OF.1213), including Alférez Guillermo Martínez (C-314) and TT Daniel Paredi (C-318) – the leader of which (Capitán Eduardo Almoño) aborted prior to take-off. Because both formations received incorrect information about the position of the KC-130H both flights returned to San Julián at 13:30 without reaching the islands.

COAN's Strike on HMS *Antelope*

For 23 May 1982, 3° Escuadrilla of the Argentine Naval Aviation originally planned a mission including four aircraft (with a fifth serving as reserve) against a ship reportedly sailing close to the mainland, to the east of the Magellan Strait. However, when Beech B-200 serial number 4-G-43 flew reconnaissance of the target, it identified it as a friendly merchant vessel. Therefore, at 12:30 a new order arrived to attack ships in San Carlos Bay. A flight was formed including CC Castro Fox (3-A-301), CC Zubizarreta (3-A-306), TN Oliveira (3-A-305) and TN Benitez (3-A-302). They refuelled from an Air Force KC-130H but Oliveira then aborted due to multiple technical issues. The other three aircraft continued and TN Marco Benitez recalled:

Passing along Mount Rosalie, heading to the harbour, I was surprised at how high we were above the water of the Sound, I had to pull negative Gs to get closer to the water and I saw that the leader did the same, I was about 100 meters behind him and to the right and I lost sight of No.3.

Looking to the front, I saw the ships, I counted four, of which the ones to my right were warships, the leader made a slight turn and headed with his aircraft to the bigger one and I saw it was a County class destroyer [in fact it was HMS *Intrepid*, who fired a Sea Cat at Castro Fox, forcing him into evasive manoeuvres just as he was releasing his bombs, and thus to miss; author's note]. I went for the fourth ship, which was a Type 21 frigate, I saw her very clearly, there was no smoke, fire or any other indications of an earlier attack. When we arrived at San Carlos, to our surprise, they started to fire SAMs from the land, we saw the smoke when they were fired and then they seemed like red flares coming towards us slowly. One of them passed between two aircraft. Closer to the ship we saw the explosions of the flak and I noted that the main gun of the ship was firing against the leader.

When I realised I was in range to fire my guns, I pressed the trigger and immediately they jammed, so I changed my weapon selector and pressed the one for the bombs, noting the release of them and the nose tried to go upwards. Immediately I turned with 90° of pitch of my wings and I went to the north at very low level to hide behind the hills, then a missile passed just in front of me and I felt that I would be shot down at any moment.

All aircraft returned safely, even if individually, to Río Gallegos. Castro Fox commented:

HMS *Antelope* after being hit by A-4Bs. A bomb-hole is clearly visible below the funnel.

The standardised camouflage pattern of the FAA's A-4Bs originally consisted of olive drab (FS34088) and dark earth (FS30118) on upper surfaces and sides (mirrored on the left and right side of every aircraft), and light blue (FS35550) on undersurfaces. By 1982, this was badly worn out on most of the surviving aircraft. The aircraft with serial number C-207 was flown by Alférez Barriounevo during the attack on HMS *Coventry* on 25 May 1982, and was the last to fly in Argentina, until 1999, when it was donated to the National Aviation Museum. In this profile it is shown armed with one AN-M65 1,000lb bomb (called a Bombola within the FAA), and decorated with one kill mark for its success from 25 May 1982. Inset is shown the insignia of the V Brigada Aérea. (Artwork by Luca Canossa)

A-4B serial number C-214 was also one of the longest serving planes of the model in Argentina, retired in 1999. This artwork shows it with yellow identification markings applied to make it easier to distinguish as 'friendly' for Argentine ground forces. The inset shows a 'bombola' with its typical markings (frequently covered by graffiti applied by the ground crews). The latter was usually mounted directly on the centreline pylon, but sometimes on the TER instead. (Artwork by Luca Canossa)

The A-4B serial C-212 – the aircraft with which TT Cervera claimed two Type-21 frigates as sunk - is shown together with the most frequently used weapon of the war: a TER with three BR.250s. In addition to having their serial number (and the unit insignia) applied on the forward fuselage, below the cockpit, the A-4Bs of V Brigada Aérea had the serial repeated on the rear fuselage, and the 'last two' of the serial on the cover of the front undercarriage. The upper inset shows the A-4B serial number C-236: this received five kill markings after the war, to commemorate the total score of IV Brigada Aérea. The lower inset shows BRP.250s on a TER, typically installed on the centreline pylon. (Artwork by Luca Canossa)

A-4B serial number C-222 eventually became one of the most famous of the FAA's Skyhawks: the inset shows its front section before it underwent a major inspection at ARMACUAR, after which there was no time to re-paint it in the usual camouflage colours. This resulted in the aircraft being painted in grey (FS36307) overall and becoming known as El Tordillo (the dapple-grey horse). C-222 was flown by TT Carlos Cachón in the attack on RFA *Sir Tristram* and RFA *Sir Galahad*, on 8 June 1982, and then by Capitan Carlos Varela in the attack on Mount Kent on 13 June 1982. It is shown as armed with three BR250s mounted on a TER under the centreline. The bottom inset shows its drop tanks – which were still in their original camouflage pattern. El Tordillo made its last flight on 15 March 1999. (Artwork by Luca Canossa)

The A-4Cs of IV Brigada Aérea originally received a camouflage pattern in off white (which by 1982 frequently turned into light tan due to wear) and olive green on upper surfaces and sides, and medium grey on the undersides. The full serial was rarely applied below the cockpit on the forward fuselage: instead, the 'last two' were worn low on the fin, below the horizontal stabilators. A few retained their black 'radomes' (covering the nav/attack system instead of the earlier radar), while most received large sections of the fin and wings painted in yellow, to make their identification for Argentinean ground forces easier. The aircraft shown here was the A-4C serial number C-322: it served until 1999, when it made the last flight for this model in Argentina. (Artwork by Luca Canossa)

A-4C serial number C-318 retained its black radome, but had its yellow identification surfaces replaced with crudely applied turquoise blue once the Argentineans realised that the yellow colour did not provide sufficient contrast and thus proved hard to recognise as such by the ground troops. Several other A-4Cs – including C-321 wore similar identification markings. C-318 was lost in an accident in 1988, by when it wore a small blue map of the Islas Malvinas, in commemoration for its participation in the war of 1982. Inset is shown the insignia of V Brigada Aérea. (Artwork by Luca Canossa)

A-4Q serial number 0654 wore the callsign 3-A-301 and was the 'flagship' of 3°Escuadrilla and one of only two equipped with the VLF Omega nav/attack system. As usual for the period until 1982, it was painted in gull gray (FS16440 or FS26440) on top surfaces and sides, insignia white (FS17875 or FS37875) on undersurfaces, and wore the large unit insignia and its call-sign on the sides of the fuselage. This artwork shows it as armed for anti-ship strike, with a MER with four Mk.82s (with Mk.12 Snakeye retarding fins) under the centreline, and the usual drop tanks. (Artwork by Luca Canossa)

While the A-4Qs of 3° Escuadrilla went into combat still wearing their standard colours of gull grey and white, the experience from 21 May 1982 quickly taught the pilots about the advantages of camouflage colours during overland operations. Correspondingly, the surviving aircraft were re-painted in similar colours to the A-4Bs of V Brigada Aérea – consisting of brown (mostly FS30215, but sometimes FS10091) and green (either FS34259 or FS30118) on top surfaces and sides – though retaining their unit insignia and the call-sign on the sides, and even 3° Escuadrilla's usual black chevron on their drop tanks. This example (0655/3-A-302) is shown armed with a MER on the centreline, mounting six Mk.82 bombs with Mk.12 Snakeye retarding fins. (Artwork by Luca Canossa)

A-4Q 3-A-304 was another of COAN's Skyhawks to receive the camouflage pattern of brown and green during the war (the others were 3-A-301, 3-A-302, 3-A-305, and 3-A-306): on 3-A-309 the green colour was applied in the form of a mottled disruptive pattern in field drab (FS30118) and red-brown (FS31136), but that aircraft was not flown in combat. Notably, in the course of camouflaging its Skyhawks, the ground personnel of 3° Escuadrilla abandoned the tradition of applying the Argentine national colours over the entire ruder and top of the fin, together with the title ARA *25 de Mayo* and the serial: only a small fin flash was applied instead. This aircraft is known to have retained such colours until at least 1983: it was retired four years later and has ever since served as a monument in front of the Argentine Navy's headquarters. (Artwork by Luca Canossa)

A-4B serial number C-207, as seen at Aeroparque Jorge Newbery of Buenos Aires, shortly after its arrival in Argentina. Notable is the silver-grey overall colour of the aircraft, and large serials and national markings. (Santiago Rivas Collection)

The A-4B of Primer-Teniente Luciano Guadagnini refuelling on 1 May 1982, when he was part of Topo Flight. On 23 May he would be shot down by HMS Antelope. He hit the ship with his bomb, which exploded while an attempt was being made to disarm it, sinking the frigate.

A beautiful study of A-4C serial number C-319, while flown by Capitan Caffarati from Oro Flight, as seen while in-flight refuelling on the way into the combat zone, on 1 May 1982. Notable is the application of yellow identification markings, and two (out of three in total) BRP.250 bombs: one under the centreline, and one on the outboard underwing pylon. (Santiago Rivas Collection)

This rare photograph of an A-4C was taken at BAM Mar del Plata during a post-war deployment – by when the Skyhawks of IV Brigada Aérea were integrated into V Brigada Aérea (which is why both unit insignia were applied on this aircraft) – and not only shows the camouflage pattern of C-322 to advantage, but also the installation of the Israeli-made Shafrir Mk.II air-to-air missiles. (Santiago Rivas Collection)

Taken in the late 1970s, this photograph shows the insignia applied to 3° Escuadrilla's A-4Qs before and early during the Malvinas War. Notable is not only the application of the national insignia on the fin, but also that of black anchors instead of roundels on the wings. (Santiago Rivas Collection)

A view of the rear deck of the aircraft carrier ARA *25 de Mayo*, as seen during the crisis with Chile in 1978. Notable are six A-4Qs of 3° Escuadrilla, and four S-2E Trackers. Both the aircraft and the carrier still looked very much the same early during the Malvinas War. (Santiago Rivas Collection

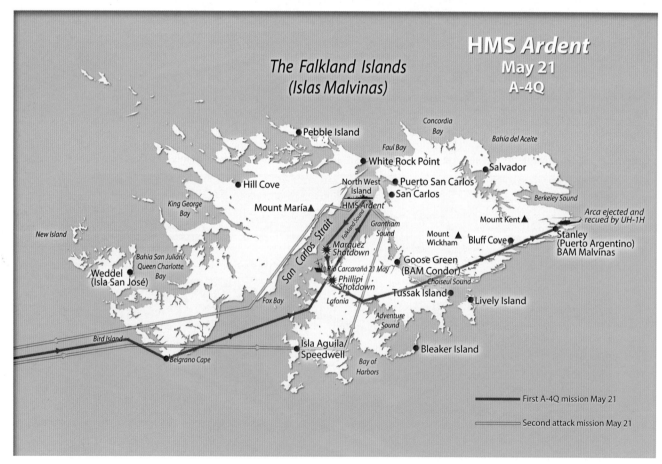

This map shows the two missions flown by A-4Qs of 3° Escuadrilla of COAN on 21 May 1982, which resulted in attacks on the frigate HMS *Ardent*. (Map by Luca Canossa)

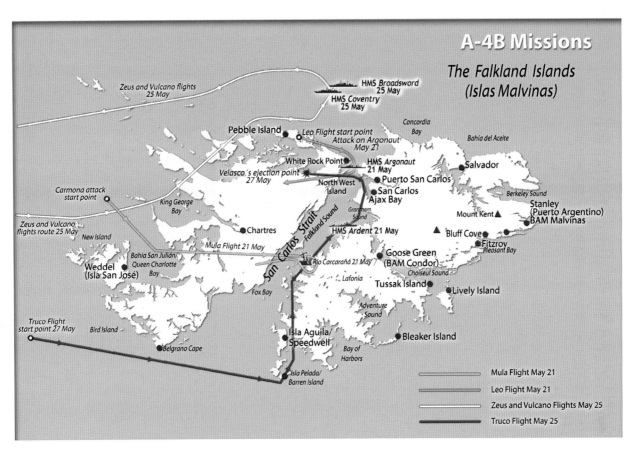

A map depicting missions flown by A-4Bs of Escuadrón II Aeromóvil on 21 and 25 May 1982. Mula Flight attacked the Argentine merchant ELMA *Río Caracana* and Leo Flight hit HMS *Argonaut*; Zeus and Vulcano flights sank HMS *Coventry* and damaged HMS *Broadsword*, while Truco Flight targeted the Royal Navy's amphibious assault and supply ships in San Carlos Bay. (Map by Luca Canossa)

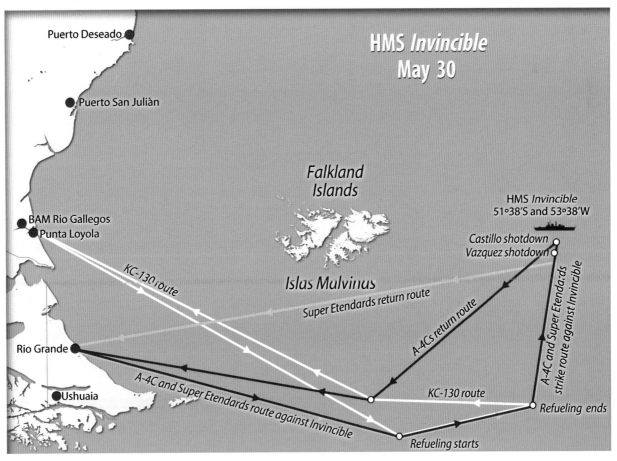

A map depicting the most complex and longest-ranged combat operation flown by the FAA during the Malvinas War, on 30 May 1982. Notably, thanks to the simultaneous deployment of both of the available KC-130Hs, the attack formation consisting of two Super Etendards (only one of which was armed with an AM.39 Exocet anti-ship missile) and four A-4C Skyhawks of Escuadron I Aeromóvil, managed to reach well to the south and then east of the Falklands and claim to have attacked the Royal Navy's carrier battle group. (Map by Luca Canossa)

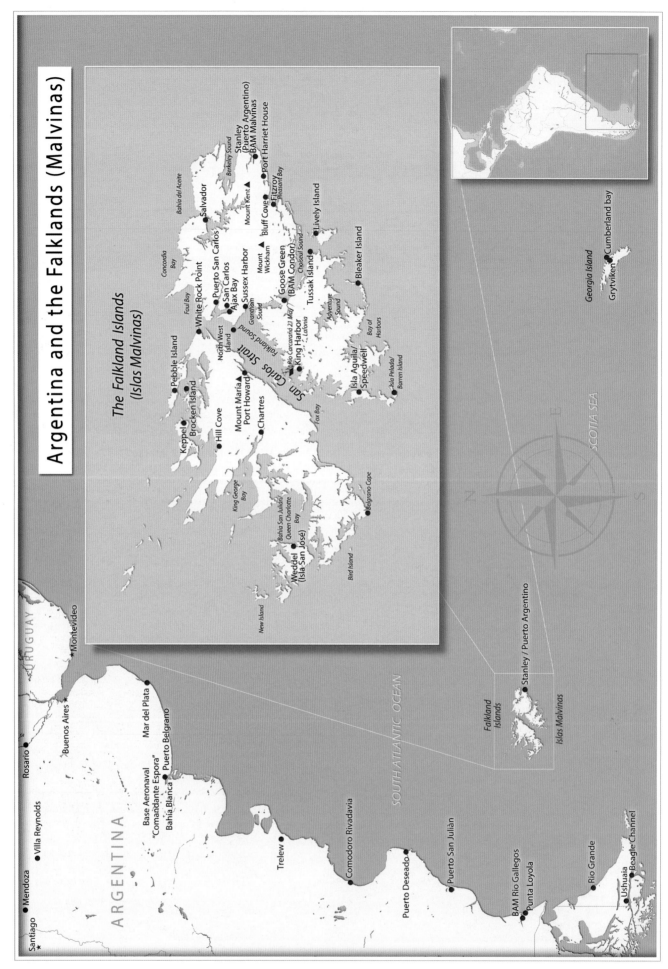

A map showing the entire combat zone of the Argentine Skyhawks during the Malvinas War of 1982, and all air bases in Patagonia used by the aircraft of CdoFAS. (Map by Luca Canossa)

Initially I attacked a Type 21 frigate which was in the middle of the bay, but I changed the target during the run as I saw one which seemed better. Close to launching the bombs I had to make a hard evasive manoeuvre to avoid a Sea Cat launched from the bow of the ship. This affected my aiming on the final part and the bomb release was when I was passing the target: thus, they fell long.

The ship attacked by Benítez was HMS *Antelope* (F170), which was also bombed by A-4Bs of the FAA. Castro Fox researched the attack, because both the Navy and the Air Force claimed the sinking as theirs. He concluded:

As the fire continued to spread during the following night, and the crew was evacuated, the magazines of HMS *Antelope* blew up in a spectacular fashion shortly before dawn, resulting in one of best-known photographs of the war.

After the airstrikes, *Antelope* had two unexploded bombs and after taking the crew to the stern, the captain, Commander Nick Tobin, ordered the disarming of both. The one that was in the air conditioning unit, close to the starboard wing, I'm sure it was the one of PT Luciano Guadagnini, of the Air Force. The second bomb entered from the port tack, close to the bridge and ended in the petty officers' mess.

HMS *Antelope*'s skipper, Commander Nick Tobin, explained:

One aircraft came straight at us. He dropped two bombs and was engaged by my starboard 20mm Oerlikon gun, which was aimed and fired by Leading Seaman "Bunny" Warren. The Aircraft was about 30ft above the water and flying very fast. One bomb flew between the mainmast and the foremast and the other hit the ship on the starboard side aft. The aircraft was hit by about eight shells from Warren's gun. It pulled up, hit the mainmast and disintegrated in a big ball of flame, scattering debris about 100 yards from the ship.[1]

Only seconds later, the ship was attacked by the COAN Skyhawks:

We opened up with the 4.5-inch gun and the Seacat. The two aircraft turned away and the Seacat missile chased them up a nearby ridge. We believe it destroyed the aircraft just over the ridge. We were then attacked again from our port side and a bomb entered the ship forward in the vicinity of the petty officers' mess. The attacks during which we were hit, were made within about one minute and it was evident they were co-ordinated and very professionally carried out.

Two Army bomb disposal experts, Warrant Officer Phillips and Staff Sgt Jim Prescott, were embarked to disarm the bombs. Tobin commented:

They were confident they would do the job. They started with the bomb aft and said they had only recently dealt with a similar bomb on another ship. It was now well after dark. They had made several

By the morning of 24 May, only the bow and stern – and a giant cloud of smoke – were left visible of HMS *Antelope*.

attempts to defuse the bomb using various methods. It exploded during another attempt and blew a huge hole in the ship's side from the water-line to the funnel. Staff Sergeant Prescott was killed in the explosion and WO Phillips lost an arm.

This story suggests that the two bombs may have been different. The experts tried to disarm first one bomb which they already knew, as they had worked with one of the same type earlier, as Castro Fox explains, this seemed to be the one from Guadagnini.

Castro Fox attacked HMS *Intrepid* and his bombs fell into the sea. According to ship's crewmember Martin Dunkin MEM(L)1:

Something hit the ship, we never did find out what hit the side. It may either have been a bomb or a part of an Argentine aircraft that was shot down over San Carlos, however when we got back to Portsmouth there were some holes in the ship's side under the waterline of one of our ballast tanks.[2]

Returning to the mainland, Zubizarreta's aircraft had a tyre blown because of the ice on the runway and while landing in a heavy shearwind. The A-4Q veered off the runway and the nose landing gear collapsed; because he still had a bomb attached, the pilot feared an explosion and ejected. His parachute failed to open completely by the time Zubizarreta hit the ground. He died a few hours later, in the local hospital.

24 May: Bomb Alley

On Monday 24 May 1982, the A-4Bs of Escuadrón II Aeromóvil were to launch a dedicated strike against the amphibious assault and support ships inside San Carlos Bay. Furthermore, in coordination with CdoFAS, the pilots decided to change their approach route to one via Ajax Bay, in order to avoid the Sea Harriers and the warships within Falkland Sound/San Carlos Strait.

The first aircraft to depart were A-4Bs of Chispa (OF.1223) and Nene (OF.1224) flights. The first was composed of TT Oscar Berrier (C-212), Alférez Moroni (C-226) and TT Luis Cervera (C-215); the second of Vicecomodoro Manuel Mariel (C-214), TT Mario Roca (C-237) and PT Héctor Sánchez (C-204). Each was armed with a single Mk.17 and took off at 9:10 in the morning. After refuelling, while connecting the armament panel, the bomb of TT Berrier was inadvertently released, so he returned to base and the other aircraft joined Nene Flight. Approaching the islands, Vicecomodoro Mariel alerted the escadrille about a ship ahead and the aircraft began the attack, but seconds after this they realised it was a rock. The aircraft flew over Barren Island/Isla Pelada and then continued over Lafonia, flying over the eastern part of the islands until reaching Choiseul Sound, where they turned north and then to the east, flying along Wickham Hill to approach Sussex Harbour before turning northwest to arrive at Ajax Bay/Rivadavia from the south. They were seen by the troops of 2 PARA, but these did not have time to alert anybody. Cervera recalled:

I saw Vicecomodoro Mariel pulling up to overfly a small mountain, and when he was over the peak I heard in the headset a laconic 'They are there'. Instinctively, all of us pushed the throttles to the limit, going still lower over the rocky terrain, looking for the best ingress to San Carlos.

I flew over the last hills and then, as in a giant theatre, San Carlos Bay appeared before my eyes, and the show was terrific! There were 10 or 12 ships on the calm waters, all forming the base for a cone of red tracers. The thought that nobody would leave alive from this hell flashed through my mind. After passing over the hilltops that surrounded the bay, I went down, literally scraping them and applying some negative g, which was uncomfortable but necessary when performing such terrain-masking manoeuvres. While doing this I lost sight of the preceding Skyhawks, then I reached the water and flew as low as I could. I was going at about 500 knots, and my big dilemma was to choose a ship as a target for my bombs. Soon I saw what seemed like an amphibious landing ship that was big enough and I went for it. All my attention was concentrated on the

View of San Carlos Bay from the south, full of Royal Navy warships – a similar view to that which the Skyhawk pilots had in their attacks of 24 and 27 May.

target which, despite being relatively near, [didn't seem] to get any closer because the AA fire was getting thicker by the moment and the tracers were passing very near and producing big splashes on the water; all this increased my anxiety to reach the target.

When I was 5ft over the water and 100m from the ship, two A-4Bs crossed in front of me and launched their bombs, which hit the water a few meters away from 'my' ship's hull.

At the height I was flying, the ship seemed very tall, and I was so close it seemed that I would hit it. I decided it was time to pull back the control stick against my stomach, while at the same time I pressed the bomb release button. Relieved of the 1,000lb weight, the Skyhawk lurched upwards, and I passed over the helicopter deck almost scraping the rails. Over the ship I banked for 90° and tightened the turn as much as possible; when I was 90º off the previous heading, I brought back my A-4 to level flight and pulling negative gs I descended to sea level. It was then that I saw two 'things' pass by my right side flying faster than I was and leaving small plumes of smoke, and both blew up against the hillside. I assumed they were missiles. When I reached the hills I had to overfly the exit from Bomb Alley I heard my wingman say in panic 'I'm hit! They've got me'. I ordered radio silence and instructed that if he decided to eject, to report over which place in order to alert the rescue forces.

Mario Roca recalled his first combat sortie as follows:

We entered from the south, there was a stream and suddenly we found the bay. I remember those who were on the stern of the ship, I do not remember if the ship had a crane, or the colour, or if it had a large structure, I remember those who were on the back and who was burning fuel because it was throwing smoke. Clearly I remember how we crossed in flight with the other aircraft, we were already accelerating, I was in front of Mariel. It was the only second I looked down. When we entered San Carlos we went down and we flew very close to the water, they were in an awkward position, Mariel said 'there they are'. I had the helmet cable pressed with the harness belt and I did not hear anything. I realised at the start, when I wanted to turn my head to see the ship, I saw another ship and then I realised, as I did not hear anything I realised it was the cable and there I coupled it and then I heard the communication mess. It must have been 15 seconds after I left the ship, I heard Mariel asking to be quiet. Because one said he wanted to reference something, something like they launched a missile. I hid with the coast, turned to the left. Everyone had a different experience. We

A Skyhawk dashing away under fire from British
air defences, low over San Carlos Bay.

landed where the Hercules were in Río Gallegos and there were the
intelligence people to make reports, which were individual. After
the interrogation ended, one told us 'you all have a different story'.
We did not agree even on the colours. That is why the perception of
intelligence is so important.

For Moroni, this was also his first combat sortie:

… a large force of the Fuerza Aérea Sur was [committed] against the
part of the fleet that was disembarking in San Carlos Bay. We left
Río Gallegos [in] two escadrilles of three aircraft, we refuelled and
then the leader of my flight returned because of a failure. I stayed
with number three, that was Cervera, and we just saw the other
flight that was behind us pass by, we leaned on that one and made
a flight of five aircraft. We descended to low level, we [passed] the
islands by the south and we did the attack from east to west. At the
time of the low level flight, as a matter of survival, I was forming
[on] them all, because I was going as a fifth plane. I was maintaining
some type of formation, but I was dodging the terrain, I entered as
the last aircraft in the bay.

The entry images are photographs that I have in my mind. When
I entered the first aircraft had already entered a few seconds ago,
[that] was Vicecomodoro Mariel and I have images of the enemy
shooting at us. I felt a strange blow on the plane, I thought it was an
impact, but then I realised that it had been the blast of one of the jets
from the front. I informed the flight leader, we made radio silence
and I settled down. The fire was usually from the right, so I placed
the aircraft as if to escape that fire, I instantly thought that I was
giving too much surface to the artillery, so I turned and aimed at a
landing craft, I fired on it, the guns did not [work], only once during
the war I was able to shoot in all the missions I did. I jumped, I saw
many ships on the right, I even remember that there were one or
two ships that did not have the format of warships, maybe [one] was
the Uganda hospital ship. We escaped, in front I jumped some small
peninsulas, there was no way to know the impact of the bomb, it
was a Mk.17. It was the only mission I did with that type of bomb.
This landing craft was very close to the coast and I saw people on
the coast. There was a settlement. I jumped the ground, I made the
escape without seeing anybody, later we made contact. I crossed
over the other island and in the middle of it I started to climb. We
all returned to Rio Gallegos. We found out that we had all returned
when we started to have contact with the radar, meanwhile we flew
in radio silence.

Héctor Sánchez concluded:

On that day I had radio problems while we were [out]going and

Luis Cervera and Héctor Sánchez at Río Gallegos.

I had to turn [the radio] off, because [it] was constantly emitting
and we could be discovered very [easily]. I was No. 3 in my flight.
When we saw the hills to the south of San Carlos, I saw the first two
[aircraft] climbing them and the leader saw the ships and informed
the rest. Then all pulled the throttle to full power, but because I
had no radio I stayed behind until I reached the top of the hills
and saw the ships. I saw two of the aircraft going for a logistic ship,
leaving some other ships behind. I descended and watched the AA
fire, they were firing with everything, missiles, guns, they were
also firing at me and it seemed as [if] all bullets will hit my plane,
miraculously I passed through them. The guys from the Navy had
said that when we were in the middle of the ships they will stop
firing because of the risk of hitting the other ships; this wasn't true,
they were firing all the time from everywhere. I first saw a small
ship and then, to the right of the logistic ship my two wingmen
were attacking, was another very big [ship], so I went for it. The
remaining two aircraft went to the right and I didn't see them.
When I selected the target, I [checked] the weapons and armed my
bomb: it was a Mk.17. When I was close to the ship I launched my
bomb, jumped the ship and then I went down, very close to the
water and turned left, heading for San Carlos, trying to fly over the
zone with less ships. I escaped very low, without seeing the others.
Then I thought "I'm safe, they will not shoot any more", but then I
saw a big explosion on the water, it must be a missile or a big gun. I
returned flying over Gran Malvina before starting my climb, I saw
another aircraft and approached. I don't know who [it] was, but he
guided me till landing at Río Gallegos. Fortunately, on that mission
all of us returned. It was a very nice mission. I'm sure I hit my ship,
close to the bow.

Indeed, the entire formation returned without major problems.
The ships they attacked were RFA Sir Lancelot (L3029), RFA Sir
Bedivere (L3004), and RFA Sir Galahad (L3005). Each was hit by one

An A-4B, probably C-237 flown by Mario Roca, darting low over San Carlos Bay after his attack on 24 May.

Another A-4B from Nene Flight streaking low past one of the Royal Navy's Landing Ship Logistics, immediately after its attack.

Bombs exploding in the water near one of the Royal Navy's Landing Ship Logistics on 24 May 1982.

bomb, but all of these failed to detonate: still, a small fire that erupted on board *Sir Lancelot* rendered her non-operational for the rest of the war, while *Sir Galahad* was out of service until the bomb was disarmed. Sailors of the Royal Navy returned fire with their small arms and at least one Blowpipe from RFA *Sir Bedivere*, while HMS *Fearless* and HMS *Argonaut* fired one Sea Cat each, all of which missed. More importantly, the pilots of Escuadrón II Aeromóvil concluded with satisfaction that – thanks to the selection of a new route – not a single British ship detected the aircraft of Chispa and Nene flights before it was too late.

Bad Luck

Following its rather inauspicious start to the war, 24 May was the day on which Escuadrón I Aeromóvil – and thus IV Brigada Aérea – finally achieved its first success. Certainly enough, the first two flights were forced to abort early: Halcón Flight – including Capitán Pierini (C-314), TT Méndez (C-322) and PT Ureta (C-310) – launched at 09:30 under OF.1228, the mission being to attack amphibious ships in San Carlos Bay with three BRP.250s each. However, only minutes before reaching its target, the formation sighted a pair of Sea Harriers high above them and aborted. Ingressing ten minutes behind was the pair that included TT Ricardo Lucero and TT Oscar Cuello (OF.1229): this formation was forced to abort in the face of massive volumes of anti-aircraft fire put up against them.

The third formation of A-4Cs, Jaguar Flight (OF.1230) launched at 10:00. It included PT Vázquez (C-324), Alférez Martínez (C-318) and TT Bono (C-305), all armed with three BRP.250s. The trio reached San Carlos Bay about one and a half hours later to promptly attack RFAs *Fort Austin* (A386), *Resource* (A480), and *Stromness* (A344). Although all pilots

A trio of Escuadrón I Aeromóvil's A-4Cs – all bombed-up and ready for action – at BAM San Julián, together with a row of Pucaras.

Another view of three A-4C Skyhawks at San Julián: all were armed with BR.250 bombs. Notable are their drop tanks painted in grey overall – obvious replacements for those jettisoned during earlier combat sorties.

An A-4C – probably the aircraft flown by Jorge Bono – as seen while distancing after its attack on warships of the Royal Navy on 24 May 1982.

After receiving a hit from ground fire, TT Bono's A-4C began streaming fuel. (Photo by James O'Connell)

eject because he was losing too much fuel and it was obvious that he could not return to the mainland. The pilot responded that he still had 3,000 pounds of fuel, turned to heading 260 and started a climb. Then they saw a ship and felt forced to descend: crossing to the south, and while about five kilometres to the south of Fox Bay, Bono re-checked his fuel status and realised this was down to 1,500 pounds (the Number 2 still had 2,280 pounds and the Number 3 about 2,500 pounds). On reaching King George Bay, C-305 entered a descent and Vázquez again ordered Bono to eject: the pilot did not answer before crashing into the sea. Because all the surviving Skyhawks were losing a lot of fuel, KC-130 serial TC-70 flew over 96 kilometres (60 miles) towards the islands to find the formation and save the remaining aircraft: the leader made contact when down to less than 200 pounds of fuel, and the Number 2 while at 1,200 pounds. The tanker essentially towed the two Skyhawks, refuelling them repeatedly until they were 30 miles from the base, where both landed safely at 13:00. After the mission, the pilots were informed that they attacked the frigate HMS *Arrow*, but this ship was not damaged on that day. To replace C-305, later the same day Escuadrón I Aeromóvil received A-4C serial number C-312.

The 'All-Out Attack' of 25 May

Nearly all of the British publications about this war point out that because 25 May was the Argentine National Day, CdoFAS went to great lengths to prepare a special effort to attack the Royal Navy's warships: indeed, that it planned to run an 'all-out offensive on this special day.' Ever since the publication of their first, semi-official account of this conflict, the Argentines have flatly denied any such claims: their heavy losses and continuously decreasing number of sorties launched are supportive of this version.[3] Indeed, there is no evidence of CdoFAS preparing any kind of special

pressed their attack home, their bombs missed: in turn, all received damage from small arms fire and began losing fuel. Three minutes after the attack, while on heading 210, the leader ordered TT Bono to

A-4C C-234 flown by TT Vázquez as seen only seconds after his attack on 24 May. Just visible bottom centre is the Skyhawk of Alférez Martínez. (Photo James O'Connell)

C-324 of TT Vázquez escaping after his attack on 24 May, as seen from the Sussex Mountains. (Photo James O'Connell)

Weapons specialists setting fuses on a trio of BF.250 bombs installed on a TER under the centreline of an A-4.

plan for 25 May 1982: it continued issuing orders following the tactics adopted in the previous 36 hours – which was to attack amphibious assault and supply ships: the sole exception was another airstrike by Exocet-armed Super Etendards. That said, there is no doubt that the crews of the Royal Navy's warships and various requisitioned support vessels (STUFT –Ships Taken Up From Trade) were advised to expect the Argentine forces to make a major effort. Therefore, not only did the Royal Navy's carrier battle group move closer to the island than it had been since 4 May (by dawn, HMS *Hermes* was only 80 miles/128km from Port Stanley, thus enabling its Sea Harriers to remain on station for much longer than usual): the 'Type 42-22 combo' was positioned north-east of Pebble Island/Borbón Island, while all the ships inside San Carlos Bay – now including RFA *Fort Austin*, RFA *Stormness*, and RFA *Resource* (A480) – were re-anchored.

The first A-4 formation to get airborne on the morning of 25 May belonged to Escuadrón II Aeromóvil, which dispatched Marte Flight (OF.1232) from BAM Río Gallegos at 08:10. This included Capitán Palaver (C-244), TTs Daniel Gálvez (C-250) and Autiero (C-221), and Alférez Gómez (C-209). Each aircraft was armed with a single Mk.17. The second pair was forced to abort: Number 3 had technical problems, while Number 4 lost the other aircraft in the dark. Palaver and Gálvez refuelled without problem and reached the northern side of West Falkland/Gran Malvina. Trying to reach San Carlos from the north, they entered a zone with bad weather and thus returned to their initial point at 09:10. From there, they flew low over White Rock Point/Punta Roca Blanca, turned right and thus reached San Carlos. The first ship both pilots saw was the white-painted SS *Uganda*: this was a hospital ship and thus both pilots passed by without opening fire. Streaking low into what they thought was San Carlos, they next saw a green ship with black hull, but flashed by before being able to set up an attack. The two Skyhawks then passed by Goose Green, where Palaver fired his cannon at a ship (which was SS *Monsunen*, used by the Argentines), while Gálvez mistakenly fired at friendly troops in the settlement. The anti-aircraft artillery at BAM Cóndor was still active and opened fire, hitting the lower part of Palaver's A-4B: he began to lose fuel but remained airborne. Meanwhile, both pilots were convinced they were over San Carlos, and they decided to split: Palaver turned north, and Gálvez south. While leaving Falkland Sound/San Carlos Strait, Palaver passed by the '42-22 combo' consisting of HMS *Coventry* and HMS *Broadsword*. The destroyer fired two Sea Dart SAMs, one of which hit and blew up the A-4B, killing Palaver. Gálvez returned safely to Río Gallegos.

Exchanging Blows

If Escuadrón I Aeromóvil had no luck thus far in the war, 25 May made no difference. The unit launched only one mission: Toro Flight (OF.1235), consisting of Capitán Jorge García (C-304), TTs Ricardo Lucero (C-319) and Daniel Paredi (C-312) and Alférez Isaac (C-302) at 11:30. After refuelling from KC-130 serial number TC-70 they continued to San Carlos, arriving there at 12:25. When they entered San Carlos Bay the British defences opened fire and immediately hit C-319 (possibly with a Sea Cat from the frigate HMS *Yarmouth*, or a Rapier launched by T Battery of the 12th Air Defence Regiment). Lucero managed to eject only seconds before his aircraft crashed into the sea and was rescued by a landing craft from HMS *Fearless* (L10). Isaac recalled:

Garcia and me were all that was left of our original flight, and thus they added Paredi and Lucero to us. It was an attack mission [against] the fleet in San Carlos Bay. After planning we got in a Ford F100 that we had from San Julián airport [and drove] to the bunkers where the aircraft were and I told Garcia: "We have a problem. Lucero is in the flight plan as 4 and I as 2. Lucero should be 2 and I should be 4". We changed positions on the truck. We took off, we did the refuelling, we started the descent as we had to be very low over Isla Del Águila, which was located south of Isla Soledad and from there we had to aim for San Carlos, that is, to the left was the strait and the flight was practically on the Malvinian coast; it was a sunny day, light blue sky. I remember it in great detail, I remember even the sheep, as they ran forward, somehow there is a wave ahead of the aircraft by a few meters and already in the distance we saw the sheep that began to run. I remember seeing the small houses they had as shelters on the islands, that they had food in case they got bad weather and stayed there. These precarious facilities were used by some pilots who ejected, [for] food and shelter.

Lucero added:

Taken from RFA *Stromness*, this photograph shows a bomb exploding near RFA *Resource* on 24 May.

TT Lucero guarded by British troops while inspected by paramedics, minutes after being captured.

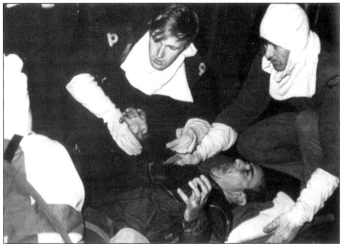

Paramedics of the Royal Navy attending TT Ricardo Lucero. He survived being shot down and captivity but died in an accident in 2010.

Just over Isla Soledad we were sure the enemy hadn't detected us and through my windshield I saw growing in front of me the mount behind which was our target. The last time I looked into my navigation system, only forty seconds remained to the combat zone. It was impossible they could intercept us. Following the terrain, we started to climb the hill to pass [over] it and once on the top we saw ahead and about 200 meters below: San Carlos Bay with six or seven enemy ships. Captain García said "There they are, to the front, come on!" We had to descend, very low over the water, and select a target. I turned my aircraft to the left and flew lateral to the enemy, before seeing a frigate to my right, with its bow pointed at me. I banked and turned towards it, fearing to touch the water with my wing. Rolling out, I pressed the trigger of my guns but they did not fire: then the British opened fire at me. I climbed a little bit and then dropped my bombs. Then I flew away.

Isaac continued:

When we arrived over San Carlos and lowered the nose, they fired with everything. The place was full of ships and each of us chose one. As I was the one on the left I saw a ship that was alone. I lowered my nose and fired the guns, 120 shots until I got low: then I put the ship in my sight and pressed the bomb button, I jumped over the ship and on the other side I climbed to avoid a hill. After that I moved the rudder down and I felt safe. During all that final run they threw everything at us: detonations of anti-aircraft fire were all around me, even though they didn't hit. After I passed the hill I turned to the right and announced that I had left the target zone. Paredi said, "Number 3 left for Puerto Argentino without news", Garcia said, "I came out but have [a] hydraulic light on". This was an intermediate emergency, but an emergency in the end. We called for Number 2, but he didn't answer. I saw Paredi in front and said "I have the 3 in sight". We called again, but neither García nor Lucero answered us. When we distanced from the islands we started the ascent to refuel. In that climb Paredi saw me, he approached and said "you [still] have the bombs on": my bombs failed to separate. Unsurprisingly, my aircraft was consuming more fuel than it should have, and I decided to eject [the stores]. We were already very high and far from improving my situation I made it worse, because the anti-return pipes that join the fuel tanks with the aircraft were cut and I started to lose fuel. I reached the tanker when down to about 400 pounds, but the tanker towed me back to San Julián. We landed and they were surprised when I opened the cabin and they saw it was me, because they said '1 and 2 would not come back' and for everybody – the Number 2 was me.

Lucero concluded:

In the moment I flew over the frigate [in fact it was HMS *Fearless*; author's note], I felt a strong impact on the lower part of the nose of my A-4. To the side of my canopy I saw big parts of what was the nose of my plane, and then the aircraft began to shake violently. The other members of my formation flew away, although I was on maximum power. I attempted to call the leader to let him know I was hit. Then I realised my radio was not working. I watched the performance indicator and concluded I was losing height. Then my controls went soft and were hardly responding. I could only keep the aircraft levelled with the stick fully to the right and back. The cockpit began to fill with smoke and I felt strong vibrations in the engine. My aircraft wasn't flying anymore and could explode, so I decided to eject. I closed my eyes and pulled the ejection handle. First, I felt the pressure from the air getting into the cockpit, then I heard noises and the rocket of my seat began to boost me upwards while I had the sensation I was rolling backwards without control.

Isaac, Paredi and García attacked frigates HMS *Plymouth* and HMS *Arrow* without scoring any hits. Indeed, García used only his guns because his bomb-release mechanism malfunctioned. On their return they were detected by HMS *Broadsword*, which, together with the destroyer HMS *Coventry*, was still to the north of Pebble Island /Punta Roca Blanca, protecting the northern entry into Falkland Sound/ San Carlos Strait. Using a data-link, the frigate downloaded the target information to *Coventry*, which obtained a lock on and fired a single Sea Dart surface-to-air missile: the weapon went straight for the aircraft flown by Captain Garcia, scoring a direct hit. The pilot ejected but nobody was aware of this and thus nobody ever looked for him. One year later his body was found in a dinghy on the beach of one of the Jason Islands. Meanwhile, C-302 of Alférez Isaac was leaking fuel, so he asked KC-130H TC-69 for help and the tanker approached the islands again and towed him back to Argentina, transferring 9,000 pounds of fuel to his Skyhawk and 1,000 pounds to Paredi. The two survivors landed only at 14:30.

Strike on HMS *Coventry*

When TT Daniel Gálvez and then the Argentine observation post on First Mountain reported the presence of the two Royal Navy warships north of Pebble Island /Punta Roca Blanca, CdoFAS quickly developed a plan to attack. The reason was not only had they killed Palaver and then Garcia, but also that they were effective at vectoring Sea Harriers into intercepts of other formations: for all practical purpose, the two warships were a thorn in the Argentine side.[4] Eventually, Escuadrón II Aeromóvil launched two flights: Zeus, armed with two BRP.250s, including TT Velacso (C-212), Alférez Barrionuevo (C-207), and TT Carlos Ossés (C-204); and Vulcano, armed with one Mk.17 each, including Capitán Carballo (C-225), TT Rinke (C-214), and Alférez Carmona. After a flight of 240 miles, Carmona was forced to abort due to a problem with his VHF system. The other aircraft reached Pebble Island with a two-minute separation between the two flights at 15:20, sighted their targets and turned to attack. Carballo recalled:

Our targets were two radar picket ships, about 30 kilometres to the north of Borbón Island. I flew along the north coast of Gran Malvina and to my left, slightly behind and below was my 'Iron Wingman' as I called TT Rinke. Suddenly I heard the voice of 'Ranquel' (Vicecomodoro Arturo Pereyra of Malvinas CIC) saying, "Attention, there is a CAP approaching from the south, over San Carlos Strait". I realised I could reach the target before they could intercept me, so I decided to follow on.

Once I turned over the island I headed east. The nose of my aircraft searched on the horizon [for] the place where the target must be. There they were, a Type 42 and a Type 22. I pulled the throttle lever and pushed the VHF button to say "Viva la Patria!" and started my bomb run. I remember I felt very small approaching with my wingman as my only company, attacking two big ships, which opened fire upon us already while we were still outside the range. I thought I was in the middle of a naval battle movie. The fire curtain was really dense and both ships were firing with all they had, which helped me to not see how close the bullets were passing.

My wingman asked "which of them are we going to attack?", "Let's go to the one which goes back, which is less defended" I answered. I remember that when I dropped my bomb, the other ship was still firing at me, both ships began to accelerate and headed to the east, separated about 200 meters from each other, one behind the other. When the ship appeared on both sides of my [salt-]covered windscreen, I pushed the trigger of my bomb and released it. Immediately I asked "Did you pass?" and heard "Yes sir, I'm behind you and in visual". Immediately I heard on the radio a voice from the other flight, saying "I have the target in visual and I'm going in."

From left to right, Carballo, Carmona, Cachón and Rinke.

Captain Pablo Carballo boarding a Skyhawk.

Carballo's flight damaged *Broadsword* with one bomb that ricocheted off the sea to smash through the hull and upwards through the helicopter hangar, ripping off the nose of a Sea Lynx helicopter in the process, before crashing into the sea – all without detonating. The British crews were to have no respite, then only seconds later Zeus Flight begun its attack, as recalled by Velasco:

We left Río Gallegos and made an air refuelling at medium height, then we descended to 20,000 feet and later we started to descend to reach the islands in very low flight over Goicoechea, which is on the south-west end of the archipelago. From there we flew directly to Borbón Island, our route indicated a line from that island to a point where we had the positions of the ships. We passed slightly to the west of Borbón Island, at about 20 or 30 meters from the water and from then on we descended as low as we could.

Carballo was one minute ahead, I couldn't see him and we were on radio silence: we only talked on the final run. We were flying over the sea toward the position given, the ships were about 30 miles from the coast, it was a sunny day, with very good visibility. Barrionuevo was to my left and he said "to the left, at nine or ten", so I looked to that side and I saw the contours of the ships against the horizon. When we turned, we climbed, as we usually did when we were flying too low, so to avoid the wing hitting the water. I think that was when they detected us, because when we finished our turn I saw a smoke cloud on the bow of the *Coventry*, the smoke of a missile and at the same moment I heard Rinke shouting "look out, a missile!" Rinke and Carballo were leaving the attack after hitting *Broadsword*. I started to follow the missile watching the fire from the engine like a blowtorch, a light flying too low, then I saw the contrail, which gave me an idea of its heading, so to manoeuvre and know if the missile was coming for me or not. We finished our turn, descended and then again we turned about 90 degrees. When I finished this second turn I saw that the missile did not track, so I turned again towards the ships and saw the missile passing, to my right, at about 500 meters from my aircraft: its engine stopped and it was nodding.

We continued our attack and on getting closer to the ships we saw the impacts on the water of the shots from their guns. The ship did many manoeuvres and my last sight was of her side: I recall watching a very big antenna when dropping my bombs. The aircraft became lighter and I jumped over the ship and Barrionuevo said "They exploded very well!" He saw the initiators, when the delay was activated with a spark: two bombs hit below the bridge, just above the water line, and one hit the main deck. Then he also passed over the ship, but his bombs failed to separate. We then flew evasion manoeuvres, all the time remaining very low. The *Broadsword* was to the right and behind: she was attacked a minute later and was damaged. The ships were one behind the other, on the same course, heading south-west, we attacked diagonal to them, from the bow.

When we left, we flew very low for a long time: we had enough fuel. Then Barrionuevo said "I lost you". I had just begun climbing and reduced power, so he could get closer but he still said that he couldn't see me, so I reduced power and then I saw him in my mirror. When he formed on me I saw something strange below his plane. I thought they were the TERs [Triple Ejector Racks], but he was returning with all three of his bombs. The problem was that he was consuming more fuel and could not return to the base. I think that the problem was that the landing gear command has a safety lock to avoid the bombs being dropped while landed, but sometimes it didn't work well. He disconnected the weapons panel and connected it again and finally the bombs fell into the sea.

We returned directly to the base, it was about one hour of flight. When we landed, there was some information on the base that the ship was destroyed, I think it came from a spotter or by the interception of the British communications. Maybe from Borbón Island they saw the smoke. We had all the best conditions for the attack, good weather and

Captain Carballo in the cockpit before a mission.

surprise. When we attacked, they fired with everything they had, I only saw the Sea Dart, I saw the hit in the water, but no aircraft was hit. You cannot hear them, you only felt them when they hit the aircraft.

Lieutenant-Commander Graham J. Edmonds, Operations Officer and Squadron Warfare Officer of HMS *Broadsword*, recalled:

Around 18:00GMT, two pairs of Skyhawks attacked us. We knew their weapon load from intelligence, and had detected the raid one

Famous photograph showing A-4Bs flown by Captain Pablo Carballo (centre, level with the horizon) and teniente Carlos Rinke (right, below the horizon) while attacking HMS *Broadsword* on 25 May.

HMS *Coventry* as seen shortly after the deadly attack. Clearly visible are two holes in the hull side, directly below the bridge (left side of the photograph), and the black identification insignia painted down the funnel and the hull of the ship to distinguish her from her two sisters in Argentine service: these proved excellent aiming points for FAA's A-4 pilots.

After the explosion of at least two of Velasco's BR.250 bombs, HMS *Coventry* began rapidly listing to port.

Wearing life vests, the crew abandoned the ship over the starboard side, and went into the inflatable rafts to be rescued by HMS *Broadsword*.

who'd seen us and called in an airstrike. *Coventry* moved the CAP south towards San Carlos ready to meet them. But then the first two aircraft contacts appeared on my radar just south of us over Mount Rosalie. I transferred the target data to *Coventry*, and the crew there forwarded them to other ships. Then there was nothing else to do but to wait for them to attack us.

Radio Supervisor Stewart A. MacFarlane served on board HMS *Coventry*:

Four Skyhawks came at us very low over West Falkland/Gran Malvina as the skipper had feared, and as expected our radars couldn't lock on because of thousands of 'land clutter' reflections. The ops officer announced, "Birds away", but instead of the usual "Targets splashed" thirty seconds later, he said, "Missed target". We fired one more missile, and then heard small arms and the 4.5-inch gun firing, so below decks we knew we were in trouble.

Edmonds continued:

We set the Sea Wolf system to the fully automatic mode, turning it into a suicide mission for the Skyhawks. We had plenty of time, with nothing to do except monitor the attack. However, the Sea Wolf had a software defect, which under certain circumstances required us to reset the system before we could fire. Imagine the horror when this defect occurred now, and we couldn't get the system on line before the aircraft came within bomb release range…!

…being only vaguely aware of the damage aft, and to avoid any further complications, [next] I had selected manual mode for our Sea Wolf. I was locked on to the aircraft when they were twenty miles away, so it was literally only a matter of time before they came within range and Sea Wolf shot them down. So, it was with some horror that we watched *Coventry* turn to starboard

hundred and eighty miles out. I talked with Coventry's air defence officer, and we agreed they would probably attack the amphibious ships. What we hadn't realised was that although Pebble Island had been attacked and neutralised, there were still Argentines there,

The last few survivors had barely been evacuated from the hull by the time HMS *Coventry* turned turtle and began the final descent into her watery grave.

The hole caused by the bomb that ricocheted of the sea surface and smashed through the side of HMS *Broadsword* while plummeting back into the water.

The Skyhawks of Velasco and Barrionuevo returning to a warm welcome from ground crews after sinking HMS *Coventry*.

The smashed nose of the Lynx helicopter on the rear deck of HMS *Broadsword*: the frigate went through six Lynx helicopters during the war, because these were all damaged during various airstrikes.

and cross our bows, coming between the incoming aircraft and us. We still weren't worried, as she'd already reported her Sea Dart system was locked on, which should mean the end of the aircraft. But when she fired her gun, we realised things weren't going so well with her either. She then crossed our line of sight to the aircraft, breaking the radar lock on, and our Sea Wolf immediately reset itself.

Two of Velasco's bombs hit the hull of the destroyer, and the third the superstructure above the main deck, close to the operations room, killing several crewmembers. Hart Dyke ordered a turn east, but the ship was rapidly losing power, and developed a 20-degree list within

minutes. The operations room was evacuated, and the crew sent up to the bridge, but the loss of electric power meant that it was impossible to even issue the order to abandon ship. Lieutenant Commander Raymond Adams continued:

A lot of people were pouring onto the upper deck; in the thick smoke there was no way you could survive between decks.

MacFarlane observed:

I returned to the communications office, then one of the officers came in and said, "Stand by to abandon ship". I hadn't realised things were that bad, but then I realised I was up to my knees in water.

Aboard HMS *Broadsword*, Edmonds watched the unfolding drama:

When *Coventry* emerged from the smoke, she looked quite normal. Then her main engines stopped and she came to a halt on the water. People were standing on the upper deck looking puzzled about what happened. But she was rapidly filling with water. The bombs had gone into the base of their fore mast, plunged down three decks into the diesel generator and engine room spaces, exploding deep down the ship, blowing a twenty-to forty-foot hole in the bilge keel.

Coventry's crew met on the starboard main deck, because the other was too close to the water and the ship was listing to that side. The eight life rafts on the starboard side were released and fifteen minutes after the attack the crew began abandoning the ship. One of the rafts was cut by the nose of a Sea Dart missile which was still on the ship's launcher and sank, and its occupants had to move to other life rafts, while another two rafts were not occupied, but turned turtle. Several helicopters were deployed from San Carlos to support the rescue operation commanded by *Broadsword*, which sent a Gemini boat to tow the rafts away from *Coventry*. As MacFarlane described:

They decided to tow us away from the ship using a Gemini assault craft with a powerful Johnson outboard. They threw us a rope but we were too heavy and the Gemini was pulled under and sank.

The helicopters rescued the people on the rafts: one picked up more than 40, and the other 15, some very badly injured. Most survivors were taken to *Broadsword*, where MacFarlane started to prepare a list of those who managed to escape:

Me and the yeoman decided we should list all the survivors, so we made a pipe for everyone to come to the communications office. We got seventy-four names. We looked at each other in total disbelief. We couldn't believe that only seventy-four out of two hundred and ninety had got off. A little bit of me died just then.

Those who could, had abandoned HMS *Coventry* within 20 minutes after the attack: the ship capsized only 7 minutes later. All four of the A-4Bs involved in the destruction of one of the most important destroyers of the Royal Navy during this war returned safely to their base.[5]

7
REGRESAD CON HONOR[1]

Bad weather impeded operations of both Escuadrón I Aeromóvil and Escuadrón II Aeromóvil on 26 May 1982. The staff and pilots of the two units thus spent the time analysing their situation. That of the former unit was particularly bad: out of 16 aircraft with which it deployed, it was down to nine, while achieving no results in return. The conclusion was clear: Grupo 4 was the least fortunate of all the Argentine fighter-bomber units. However, the war went on, and as the weather improved CdoFAS issued new orders for airstrikes on targets in the San Carlos area, and 'suspected ships underway at the entrance to Choiseul Sound'. The first to depart from San Julián was Toro Flight (OF.1248), including A-4Bs flown by PT Cachón (C-250), Alférez Gómez (C-227) and TT David Gálvez (C-240). The second formation was Tanque Flight, consisting of A-4Cs. They took off at 09:30, each armed with a single Mk.17 bomb. Half an hour later, Trueno Flight (OF.1245) including PT Filippini (C-207), Vicecomodoro Rubén Zini (C-239), and TT Autiero (C-212). Because the position of the target eventually could not be confirmed, all were ordered back to base during the IFR-operation.

These two formations were followed by four A-4Cs of Tigre Flight (OF.1246), which launched at 10:00. The latter was unusual in so far as all of its aircraft were equipped with drop tanks taken from IX Brigada Aérea's Pucara COIN-strikers (similar to Aero 10 drop tanks used on Skyhawks), and with three LAU-61 pods for 68mm unguided rockets each. The flight included Capitán Jorge Pierini (C-314), TT Oscar Cuello (C-302), and TT Ernesto Udeta (C-318). The final formation was Tanque Flight, including Capitán Eduardo Almoño (C-310), Alférez Carlos Cordington (C-301), and PT Normando Costantio (C-321), in which every aircraft was armed with three BRP.250s. Both A-4C flights refuelled from the KC-130H TC-69, but C-318 and 321 had to return because of technical problems. The others failed to find any targets and also returned with their weapons still on board.

Attacks on HMS *Fearless* and HMS *Intrepid*

During the afternoon of 27 May, two other A-4B flights were launched with the aim of striking the packing plant in Ajax Bay, used as a staging ground and a field hospital by the British Army, and on San Carlos Settlement. Poker Flight (OF.1244) launched at 15:00, including Capitán Carballo (C-207), TT Rinke (C-212), and Alférez Carmona (C-239), each armed with four BRP.250s. Truco Flight (OF.1247) followed half an hour later, composed of PT Velasco (C-215), and TTs Carlos Ossés (C-228) and Robledo: the later aborted before take-off. Carballo recalled:

Because my radio wasn't working well, I ordered Rinke to lead and make the navigation. Again, we crossed that long space of water, to start our descent and began to fly along the southern coast of Gran Malvina, passing through the south end of San Carlos Strait. At Isla Pelada, we turned to the north, following the east coast of the strait. I took charge of the navigation again. We got into Ruíz Puente after seven minutes and we saw the small hill which was the southern end of Ajax Bay. I ordered a last armament control [check] to TT Rinke, as Carmona had to return because of technical problems with his plane. It was sunset, with poor visibility and clouds. I started to climb the hill and when I reached the top I tried to follow the contour of it, trying to fly as low as I could.

Just after we appeared from the top of the hill, they began to fire at us. It was like as if someone had activated fireworks. Rinke shouted 'What do we do now?' and I replied 'go ahead Rinke'. Apparently, the soldiers on that hill started to fire at us, making a curtain of orange tracers. Meanwhile, two ships in the bay also began to fire at us.

I saw the target ahead, I looked to my left and there was a lot of activity, five Sea King helicopters were flying exactly over the place where PT Velasco would attack, he was one minute behind me. Also I saw a lot of ships, so I informed everybody about this on the radio. I arrived at the southern part of the bay and flew as low as I could over the water. In the sunset, the spectacle was beautiful; it seemed a party, not a war, lights, fires and tracers illuminating the grey bay. As we [had] planned I ordered "Up now!" and pulling our stick we climbed to reach the necessary height, "Drop now!" and the parachutes of our bombs were deployed, as my wingman would later tell me. We were flying in between a mass of bullets fired from the ground in all possible directions and covering our aircraft. For an instant I looked to the right and saw the tracers passing very close to my wingtip.

I climbed the hill which was ahead of me, following the terrain. Our bombs exploded illuminating the hills around the bay. Later I heard the "leaving" from the other flight. Then I heard Velasco saying calmly "I have hydraulic system failure lights on, apparently I was hit" and TT Ossés said "Sir, you have fire on the underside of your aircraft, close to the left wing root."

I understood that the hydraulic fluid was very flammable and that fire was exiting from below the liquid oxygen tanks, also very flammable and his aircraft was about to explode, so I ordered "Mariano, eject now!", while TT Ossés wrote his position

Ajax Bay refrigeration plant after the British landing and before the airstrike of 27 May.

The Ajax Bay plant in flames after the Skyhawk attack on 27 May 1982.

immediately. I repeated "Mariano, I order you to eject, now!" and he answered, "wait a little bit, after I cross the pool [Falkland Sound/San Carlos Strait] I will eject". Because I insisted TT Rinke shouted, "shut up, he knows what to do!" I shut up and concentrated on my own aircraft. Nothing was working, only the compass was showing my heading. Some minutes later, the radio also stopped working. Urgently I looked to my wingman through my mirror and there he was; I reduced throttle and formed with him, letting him know, by hand signals, about my problem. He indicated to form and follow him. We flew for some minutes when I watched coming ahead two aircraft flying very low, which seemed to me as being Harriers.

As I didn't have radio, I waved my wings, pulled the throttle and passed the wingman, for him to follow me. We flew by about ten

minutes at maximum power and then reduced to let Rinke pass me and take the lead. Later he told me they were two Pucarás.[2] We returned in silence, night was falling and I was flying with the fear of losing visual with Rinke, because if that happened I probably would have had to eject in the very cold and windy night.

My aircraft was hard to control on landing and tried to veer to the side: a bullet had destroyed my left wheel. I put the brakes and the rudder to the other side, trying not to break the other wheel. After I descended from the aircraft I saw the cause of the failure of my equipment: there were five impacts and a big hole in the nose, a bullet hole in the lower part of the aircraft, and another one – where the bullet stopped shortly before reaching my chest – the final two in the wheel and the engine. TT Ossés also had hits on both drop tanks.

Velasco recalled:

The procedure was as always, medium level flight, air refuelling, four 500-pound BRP bombs to be launched at no less than 30 meters. Flying very low we crossed Falkland Sound/San Carlos Strait by about the middle of its length, we passed to the other island and then we turned left to fly along the west coast of the island so to arrive at San Carlos Bay from the south. The refrigerating plant was on the left coast of the bay and on the other side was the settlement. We had to attack the former. There we saw a lot of containers, one or two helicopters, pallets, I saw everything very fast, the aircraft at full power, with four bombs, was flying at about 430 knots. When we passed the hills to the south of the bay (the Sussex Mountains), we saw everything, four or five ships. I was to the left of the two aircraft formation, we descended and approached the target flying very low. When I started to climb to drop the bombs I heard the noise of some impacts, not very loud, but I felt as if a hammer was knocking the plane. Ossés shouted "look out, a missile!" but apparently the missile passed between our aircraft and caused no damage. We had the weapons panel connected, I dropped the bombs and immediately after I heard four or five strong impacts. Immediately I heard Ossés telling me that I had fire on my plane. He was behind me. At the same moment I saw some emergency lights turning on. He told me I had fire on the left wing, I reduced throttle and then I pulled to full throttle again to note it was still working well, I heard some noises and the hydraulics and fuel emergency lights turned on. Ossés then shouted "Eject! Eject!" but I climbed and flew over the hills that separated the bay from San Carlos Strait. Then I headed west. The ship that fired against me was to my right, in the bay, and we exited to the left.

When I was flying over the strait I saw the smoke coming from my airplane in the mirror, below the flaps. I saw the coast of Gran Malvina/West Falkland/Gran Malvina and started to climb. I realised I had to drop the tanks and also I dropped the TERs, with the emergency handle I ejected everything. I reduced throttle, climbed to 1,000 feet and with 250 knots I ejected once I was flying over the island. I knew that I had Port Howard to my left, despite [that] I couldn't see it, but they heard the explosion of my plane.

I landed and immediately after I heard some aircraft but I couldn't see them, they turned about two times above me and then they headed east. I hid for some time and later I prepared my stuff and after the night had fallen I started walking. Despite that I knew there were Argentine troops in Port Howard, we had the information that maybe they had surrendered, so I headed to Fox Bay. I walked day and night, relaxing every 40 minutes, during the 28th and on the morning of 29 May I found a refuge, I had walked about 50 kilometres. It was empty but had some food stored, so I stayed there until on the 31st three islanders arrived on horses and they told me they would inform the garrison at Port Howard. On the night of the 28th I saw the combat at Goose Green, I saw flares in the sky and heard explosions. On 1 June a Land Rover arrived with an Argentine doctor and an islander driving. We went to the crash site and the islander asked me if he could take the canopy of the plane. I replied yes and we loaded it on the rear of the Land Rover, above my feet and we went to Port Howard.

I stayed at Port Howard until 6 June when the hospital ship *Bahía Paraíso* arrived. The British bombed us every night, for about an hour. I left on the ship, where I met PT Ricardo Lucero, shot down in an A-4C and rescued by the British, who later transferred him to our ship. Then we arrived at Punta Quilla, on the mainland, where we boarded a Sikorsky S-61N helicopter of Helicópteros Marinos

and we went to Port Santa Cruz. I continued to Río Gallegos and on the next day, 8 June, I boarded a Learjet to return to our base at Villa Reynolds, where I met my family.

Able Seaman (M) Neil Wilkinson, aimer of the starboard side Bofors 40mm of the amphibious assault ship HMS *Intrepid*, recalled this action:

27 May was to be a different day, no attacks throughout the day until late that afternoon. I was sat on a box of ammunition resting and enjoying the warm sun on my face, doing a word search in a magazine, my loader and supply numbers were round on the port bridge wing having a talk to the men on the other side when the alarm sounded.

I threw everything into the air and ran to the gun, flicking switches and starting the gun's motor up. The gun itself was facing forward and the ship was actually facing the way the aircraft were attacking from, I managed to fire six rounds off at the two Skyhawks and saw one of them go over the hill with smoke trailing out from behind it. I had the thumbs up from the lookouts above the bridge that I had hit one of the aircraft, I wasn't 100% sure, until we arrived back in England.

Wilkinson had hit Velasco's aircraft and although *Fearless* also claimed the kill, this ship was to the right of the aircraft's path while all the were on the left wing. *Intrepid* was ahead of the Skyhawks and Wilkinson explained he could see both wings of the aircraft from his position.

Ground Attacks

Through all of this time 3° Escuadrilla of the COAN was kept on alert but – due to problems with serviceability of its aircraft and bad weather – rarely launched. On 25 may, it planned a reconnaissance sortie to the west of West Falkland/Gran Malvina, but this was cancelled due to bad weather in Río Grande. On 26 May, TN Olmedo launched in 3-A-301 and TF Medici in 3-A-302 at 09:27. However, they found no targets and returned to base at 11:17. On landing, Medici's aircraft blew a tyre and was stopped only by the arrestor wire at the end of the runway. At 12:37, TN Rótolo launched in 3-A-301, followed by TN Oliveira in 3-A-302, for an armed reconnaissance sortie of Lively Island. They reached the KC-130H tanker at 13:00, but then encountered problems during the IFR-operation and both aborted. Another armed reconnaissance was ordered for 27 May, and at 09:27 TN Oliveira took off with 3-A-301 and TF Olmedo with 3-A-302. Although passing low over Cape Meredith and Queen Charlotte Bay /Bahía San Julián, they found nothing and returned at 11:30.

At 11:20 on 28 May, TN Sylvester departed Río Grande in 3-A-301 with TN Lecour in 3-A-302. They reached north west Rincon, but because of the very bad weather could not find any targets and thus returned without contact with the enemy. After this flight, the four remaining A-4Qs were unserviceable and the mechanics worked hard to restore them to serviceability: the job was complete only on 7 June, when TF Olmedo flew 3-A-301 and TC Médici 3-A-305 for a training flight.

Meanwhile, Cuña (OF.1254) and Nene (OF.1258) flights of Escuadrón II Aeromóvil of the FAA were ordered to attack naval targets in Grantham Sound/Ruiz Puente because HMS *Arrow* was bombarding the Argentine forces at Goose Green from the local waters. The first flight included Capitán Carlos Varela (C-204), Alférez Moroni and TT Roca (C-214), while the other comprised the aircraft of Vicecomodoro Ernesto Dubourg (C-225), Alférez Alfredo Vázquez

HMS *Invincible* as seen during its visit to Ascension Island (together with RMS *St Helena*), as the Royal Navy's task force was underway towards the Malvinas in April 1982. (Photo Bob Shackleton)

(C-226) and Lt Cervera (C-239). Nene 3 and Cuña 2 had to return and the others flew over the bay without finding a target, because the weather was very bad. At 14:30 all landed at Río Gallegos. Moroni recalled:

> Apparently, there were naval targets outside the Brenton Loch/Ruíz Puente, and they sent six aircraft. We did air refuelling, initially coming from the south, we went up the Strait of San Carlos until entering the target zone. There was very bad weather. After the refuelling one of my extra tanks did not transfer, so I was keeping all the fuel, I continued the descent and when I reached the minimum fuel the instruction was to return, because I [not only had] the bombs but the fuel that was in the tank that did not transfer. I returned a few minutes before the rest reached the target. They arrived, they toured the bay, there was bad weather, they found nothing: both flights orbited between the strait and the bay so as not to hit the land, but there was not much room for manoeuvre and they did not find anything either.

Meanwhile, the attack of the British 2 PARA on Goose Green began, supported by shelling from the frigate HMS *Arrow*. Informed about the resulting battle, CdoFAS ordered several flights into the air. Bad weather spoiled nearly all of the planning and thus only two flights of A-4Cs got airborne. The first of them launched at 13:00: Chispa Flight (OF.1259) included PT José Vázquez (C-301) and TTs Atilio Zattara (C-310) and Daniel Paredi (C-322). Although the leader had to return shortly after take-off – when, because of a failure on the armament panel, his bomb was released while connecting the panel – the other two Skyhawks continued. Ten minutes later Toro Flight (OF.1253) took off with Captain Mario Caffarati (C-321), PT Omar Castillo (C-318) and Alférez Gerardo Isaac (C-302). Isaac recalled:

> Before reaching Waypoint 1, the aircraft acting as radio relay told us there was no CAP and they gave us the target position, but wrongly. Because the Omega navigation system couldn't understand the data, we asked again and he replied he had made a mistake and gave us the right position. Although the ceiling was over 1,200 feet, visibility was of 3 miles, sometimes better or worse. After Waypoint 1 we headed to the target but when we arrived at its position we didn't find it and headed home. When we turned to 270° heading, always at very low altitude, we saw a big silhouette smoking; we informed each other about it and turned towards it. Close to the ship the leader advised it was a hospital ship, we passed to the left and headed home. When we were at about 180 miles the relay told us we had to go to the tanker and then return to the target. Toro 1 and Chispa 1 and 2 returned because they had minimum oxygen,

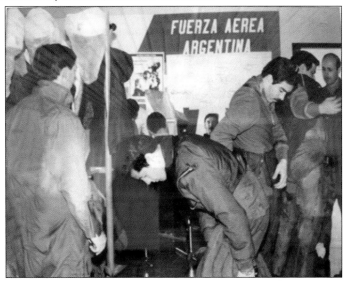

Crews preparing for the mission against *Invincible*.

continuing with the mission [with] only Toro 2 and 3. We went to the tanker and Toro 2 only loaded 4,000 pounds, but we follow[ed] with the mission to refuel on the return. When we were at 140 miles from the target we received the order to return to the tanker and wait for [further] orders. We started to turn and then they ordered [us] again to return to the target. With only 4,500 pounds of fuel we could not reach the target and thus returned to the tanker once again. When the command heard about this, they ordered us back to base.

29 May 1982 also saw little action. Only Escuadrón II Aeromóvil dispatched Oro Flight (OF.1267) – including Captain José Bergamaschi (C-212) and Alférez José Barrionuevo (C-237), armed with three BRPs each – to San Carlos. They took off and reached the target zone but found nothing. On the return they spotted a ship at 51°S/59°W (to the north of San Carlos Strait), but they didn't attack because they were low on fuel.

30 May: Heavy Seas

Since the successful Exocet-strikes on the destroyer HMS *Sheffield* (D80) and the requisitioned merchant SS *Atlantic Conveyor*, on 4 and 25 May 1982, respectively, the commander of the Royal Navy's task force off the Falklands/Malvinas, Admiral Sandy Woodward, had moved both of his aircraft carriers – HMS *Hermes* (R12) and HMS *Invincible* (R05) – well to the east of the disputed islands. Nevertheless, the operators of the FAA's AN/TPS-43 radar deployed on the islands were carefully monitoring the operations of the Sea Harriers and, by calculating their routes – concluded the approximate position of both ships at 51°38'S and 53°38'W, about 300 kilometres (186 miles) to the east of the Falklands/Malvinas. This method of assessing the position of the Royal Navy's task force was put to the test on 25 May, when two Super Etendards attacked from the north, and proved successful. Correspondingly, the idea was born to repeat the exercise, but this time from the south. This mission was originally planned for 29 May and to include just two Super Etendards, one of which would carry the last AM.39 Exocet anti-ship missile in the Argentine inventory of the time. After hearing about the COAN's planning for this operation, the FAA requested to take part: an agreement was reached and around noon of 29 May four A-4Cs of Escuadrón I Aeromóvil were re-deployed to Base Aeronaval Almirante Quijada, outside Río Grande. However, their arrival came too late for such a long-range operation to be conducted in daylight, and thus the mission was postponed to the next day. Thus began one of the most controversial missions of the war: a mission that was not only one of the most risky and longest-ranged anti-ship strikes since the end of the Second World War, but became controversial because the British insist that this attack never even reached any of the Royal Navy's aircraft carriers, while the Argentines insist to this day that they not only reached one of the two precious British warships, but also hit it with their bombs.

Mission OF.1268: Strike on HMS *Invincible*

Primer Tenientes José Vázquez (on C-301) and Ernesto Ureta (C-321) volunteered to take part, and they selected PTs Omar Castillo (C-310) and Alférez Gerardo Isaac (C-318) as their wingmen. Teniente Paredi (C-302) was to serve as a reserve. The formation was code-named Zona, and each aircraft was armed with three BRP.250s. In front of them was Section Ala, including Super Etendards 3-A-202 piloted by Capitán de Corbeta (CC) Alejandro Francisco, and 3-A-205 with Teniente de Navío Luis Collavino. Because of the long flight and the quantity of aircraft both FAA KC-130Hs were reserved for this mission, both launching from Río Gallegos. Alférez Isaac recalled:

On May 29 I was resting, I arrived in the morning, I ate, I drank with some mates and went to the infirmary, a large darkened room with campaign cots: there were no wounded, no sick, and I threw myself into one for a nap. At midday a soldier came and told me that Lieutenant Ureta was looking for me, I told him I was resting and he said it [made no difference]. As we were more afraid of Ureta than of the British, I went to see him, he told me to change, that I had to fulfil a mission. So, I started to change my clothes. While I was walking he was describing the mission. In that talk he told me that we were going to fulfil a mission that had to do with the aircraft carrier, a diversionary mission, to cause the Sea Harriers to take off and then return. We went to Rio Grande, an escadrille formed with Vásquez as 1, Castillo as 2, Ureta as 3 and I as 4.

Volunteers did not exist in the war, we were all afraid and we all had a great internal job that was to dominate the fear the way each one found for that. My method was that I was more afraid of someone seeing that I was afraid [than that] something would happen to me. I did not have to show that I was afraid and with that little game I put fear in my pocket, but I did not show it.

To make up this mission, the squadron leader, who was Vicecomodoro Juan José Lupiañez, gathered the oldest ones and told them that there was an attack mission against an aircraft carrier and that he needed two volunteers. At that question, Ureta raised his hand and said he was going, Vasquez said he would too. Lupiañez told them to choose their wingmen, Vázquez chose Castillo, Ureta chose me and Paredi as reserve, and that escadrille was put together. I pay homage to Vásquez and Ureta who did what no one did. They had the greatness to volunteer for a mission of this kind. At that time they differed from the rest. These changed the level, from then I looked at them in another way and even today when I see Ureta I see it in another way. We went to Rio Grande, we landed at noon, we went to the meeting room, they were starting flight planning that for me was a diversion, they were dictating the coordinates of the points and at one point they say "Oscar Mike", which means material objective [Objetivo Material in Spanish, which meant there was a real target and not a diversion].

Although I did not know almost anyone, next to me was Major Lupiañez, cousin of my squadron leader, who was flying Mirage III and was also the husband of a cousin of my girlfriend who is my wife today, so I knew him, I asked him and he said we were going to attack the aircraft carrier, and I said "no". While I was writing, a guy appears and says that the mission was suspended and said: "A tanker failed and it's postponed for tomorrow." I spent a day in Rio Grande, in the worst of internal situations because I already knew what was going to happen, the worst period is the vigil, once I got on the aircraft and started up, my anxiety level dropped. When I took off or was taxiing it was pure work and I never thought about what would happen to me, in flight I felt good, but on land and waiting, not.

At the base there were a lot of people, it was full of sailors, it had nothing to do with how we lived in San Julián. In the afternoon they called me and they asked me if I wanted to talk on the phone, I had 3 minutes, I called my father who was a commodore in the Air Force, he was in Buenos Aires, I could not give him any detailed explanation and he more or less knew what was happening, but he did not know it was me. At night we went to eat at the YPF Club because it was the Army Day, I sat at the table in front of Captain Janett, who had been my flight instructor at the aviation school, my mind was elsewhere, we went back to the base, where I slept, I compared it with where I was in San Julián and this was a nursing

A flight of A-4C Skyhawks, all armed with BR.250 bombs, preparing for take-off.

room.

In the morning we got up, I saw Ureta who was still resting, I stayed, at midmorning a soldier came and said they were waiting for us in Operations, we left, Vásquez and Castillo had gone to change aircraft. We went to Operations, Vásquez and Castillo were already there. There they gave us all the information to fly, we went to the airplanes and while we were walking on the tarmac Vázquez said "I will not add anything else, I only ask you to pray a Hail Mary at the head before taking off." We took our aircraft, I had C-318.

We were in Río Grande because the mission had to be done with Super Etendards and the last Exocet that was left, that was being saved for when an aircraft carrier was in range, because they were always more than 100 miles east of the islands. Of the Super Etendards, the leader was Francisco and the second was Collavino, and we went with three BR-250 bombs with smooth tail and two fuses, one on the nose and one on the tail, modified, with 12 seconds of delay.

While we started taxiing I saw the take-off of the Super

The ground crew writing "Regards to the little prince" on a BR.250 bomb, referring to Prince Andrew, who was serving as helicopter pilot on board the Royal Navy carrier.

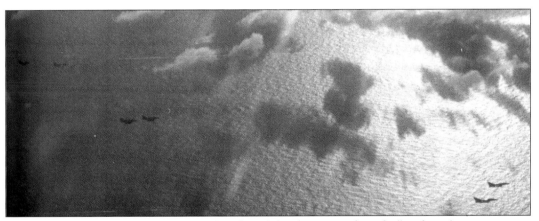

The two Super Etendards and the four Skyhawks as seen after refuelling from the KC-130H Hercules on the mission against HMS *Invincible* on 30 May 1982.

Etendards, we arrived at the runway end, we did the engine tests and we took off individually. I took off, I joined the others, we went to the tankers that were waiting for us about 100 miles south of the islands, there were the two tankers that left from Río Gallegos. When we arrived at the position they were already formed front and back, in the front they refuelled the two Super Etendards and in the back we went in pairs. Thus, we headed east for about 100 more miles, making successive refuellings en route. When we reached the final point we left the KC-130s and at that moment we were Ureta and I to the left and Vásquez and Castillo to the right, contrary to what was planned. Vázquez and Castillo had to form with Francisco, who had the missile, and Ureta and I to Collavino, who was on the right to support with the radar. The Super Etendards flew in line at a thousand meters between aircraft and aircraft and we had to form Vásquez and Castillo on the left at about 50 meters and the others on the other side. We were located the other way, I assumed it was the same, Vásquez ordered us to go over the other side, so we were formed as planned.

About 25 miles after the refuelling, we started the descent to get to heading 345, a little less than heading north. This succession of refuellings was necessary for us to go more to the east, to enter with some deviation and to increase the surprise factor. The most anticipated attack was from the west, all its few defences had to be looking to the west and not to the east. The other issue of survival was not to talk [on the radio] and the other important one was the low flight, low enough until I was afraid of hitting the water and high enough until I was afraid of getting detected by the radar.

At 40 miles from what would be the target, according to the coordinates given, the Super Etendards lifted for the first time, made a radar sweep and went down, at 30 miles did the same and at 20 the launch should occur. When they get up I look to the left to see the launch, I thought that the missile was coming out of the pylon but it fell down, when I saw that the missile was falling [and] I thought that it had failed, but then its engine started. In this moment their leader said "in front is the aircraft carrier," turned left and returned to Río Grande. We follow the trail, we start to converge and the missile disappeared in a moment, it got lost in the horizon (the weather was covered with clouds, grey with some showers that we had to avoid) and in the same place where the missile was lost, a few seconds later, the silhouette of a very large ship appeared, very different from what I had seen in San Carlos, unlike all the silhouettes we had studied and the clearest was the asymmetry, the ship was in the same direction we were flying and it was totally asymmetric, the flight deck gave me a disruptive vision, I was clearly looking at an aircraft carrier, I clearly saw the flight deck and the island where all the antennas and the bridge are, as

Alférez Gerardo Isaac's A-4C C-318 returning from the mission against HMS *Invincible* on 30 May. By this time, all the Skyhawks of Escuadrón I Aeromóvil had had their yellow identification markings overpainted with azure blue.

we approached two columns of black smoke began to emerge on both sides, as if screwed, came from both sides, more and more smoke began to settle in the area of the aircraft carrier and began to cover the lower part of her. As I got closer I started to see her only from the flight deck upwards, in this moment I started to feel hot air, I started to feel the mask very hot and I thought I had to put more cold air, but this meant that I had to take the hand from the accelerator and grab the stick with the left and with the right hand move the command of the air. I sent the command to both hands and neither responded, the left stayed on the accelerator and the right on the stick. I stuck close to the water, since I saw the aircraft carrier I forgot the rest of the world, I had what is called target fascination, I experienced it exactly as the manual says, as if two earmuffs began to close and the only thing that existed for me was the ship. Until about 10 kilometres away I felt an explosion that I knew was not from my plane, I looked to the left and saw an A-4 that was exploding, a wing broke, showed the belly and crashed on the water. Everyone was to my left, I was on the right. I did not know who it was. I looked forward again, back to the ship and when I was about to start shooting with the guns – I wanted to start shooting the guns from afar, because on May 25 when I entered San Carlos and entered shooting with guns I felt invulnerable, I felt that nothing was going to happen to me – they were firing at us, the explosive ammunition was visible. When I was about to start firing I felt another explosion, much stronger, inside the cabin. I felt it as when you let out the gas for a while and then throw a phosphorus, pressure and depression, it's the same sensation because it's not even noise. I looked to my left and saw, at between 5 and 10 meters, another A-4 that exploded, the image I have was an A-4 twice as long and twice as fat, with the same shape of the A-4 but with all the sheets separated and between sheet and sheet all orange. I looked again at the nose and began to shoot with the guns, 200 rounds came out against the stern and over the smoke, because I was flying between the flight deck and the water, up to the right was the island. I couldn't climb to pass over the deck, so I turned right and went through the right side of the aircraft carrier. When I passed the bow of the aircraft carrier I started to make turns with high load factor, right and left for a long time, trying to prevent me from being hit.

From then on, my priority was survival. When I considered

it enough I turned left to set course for escape and return to the southwest. Always looking back, because the carrier would appear to me. I looked and suddenly a whole area full of smoke began to appear, I did not see the silhouette of the aircraft carrier. At that point I began to move away and broke the radio silence. I called, no one answered me, I assumed I was returning alone and while I put my navigation stick on the horizon, in low escape, I saw a point. The first thing I thought was that it was a Harrier that came to intercept me and I did not have one more shot. The point was still in the same place, I immediately realised that it was another A-4 and I started to approach.

When I was close, the pilot raised his arm so that I started to approach him and when he raised his arm I saw that the flight suit was orange. In our squadron we shared the anti-exposure suits, as our mission was not air war but land war, I had no idea what the anti-exposure suit was until the war. There were only two American-made orange suits, one was mine and the other was used by Ureta. I knew it was Ureta, but the first thing that came to mind were Vasquez and Castillo. When I raised my arm I said "they hit Vasquez and Castillo." I could not talk, I called, but I could not communicate, until we communicated. We talked quickly about what we had seen, what we had attacked and the losses. Ureta says "we're going straight back to Rio Grande" and then he said "no, we're going to refuel," so I called the tankers.

I give them the preliminary report of the mission. Ureta went to the right hose and I went to the other tanker. He again passed all the information we had, especially the losses. We approached visual, after 3.45 hours of flight, all the people were waiting for us, when we arrived we tuned off the engine, I went down, I embraced with Ureta, I do not remember anything, but what I remember is that I could not talk to anyone, they put me in a van unable to talk to anyone, I was interrogated by Air Force intelligence, Navy intelligence, then in conjunction with Ureta, then with the two Navy pilots, to check what we had done. Brigadier Crespo (the commander of the Fuerza Aérea Sur, in charge of all the war operations) came with part of his staff, we had a meeting with him and he wanted to know what had happened and while all this intelligence was happening he told us that the aircraft carrier that we had attacked was the *Invincible*, which wasn't something that we knew, as it was clear because the flight deck was very flat. Ureta passed over it and could see it very well and the flight deck was very flat.

We did not return with the A-4s to San Julián, the LV-ALF came, which was a Learjet of the Fénix Squadron assigned to San Julián and they took us.

Ureta's Story
Ernesto Ureta recalled the attempt to hit HMS *Invincible* as follows:

The other of the two surviving A-4Cs after the attack on HMS *Invincible* was C-321, flown by PT Ernesto Ureta, and these two photographs show it while approaching the KC-130H tanker while on the way back from the mission. Notable are empty pylons and drop tanks painted in grey overall.

Ground crew applying the traditional 'kill marking' on Ureta's C-321, a day after the mission.

We approached on heading 340° or 350°, forming to the Super Etendards, at 100 feet altitude and a speed of 420 knots. Before launching the Exocet, the Super Etendards made a slight correction to the right and the wingman remained slightly ahead of the leader. I heard the leader indicating the position of the target, so I asked "how far?" and he replied "20 miles ahead."

Then I pulled the throttle to full power and I called Zonda 1, but he didn't answer, although I had him within sight: he was approaching me while we were converging to the target. Once we were at 30 meters from each other I saw that a part of his left wing detached from his aircraft: seconds later, the engine exploded, leaving the aircraft without the rear part. He began a descent to the left. I had not seen the moment in which it hit the water, nor the pilot ejecting. We were too low and I do not think he could do so.

Meanwhile, my target was in view and [I] continued my approach and when I was in range for my guns, I opened fire. However, my cannons jammed after firing only two rounds. Thus, I continued my approach keeping the pipper on the target all the time, then pressed the trigger to drop the bombs while attacking from about 30° from the stern, before passing over the rear half of the ship. Once on the other side, I called Numbers 2 and 4, but they did not answer. Thus, I assumed I was returning alone. It was only later that I saw [in] my mirror that another aircraft was to the right and behind

me: on changing the frequency of my radio to that for contacting tankers, I realised this was the Number 4.

When I recall that mission, I am sure we attacked HMS *Invincible*: it had a long island atop a long, empty flight deck. On the final leg of my attack run, I saw a lots of dense, black smoke rising from the ship. Moreover, when trying to see the ship after the attack all I could see was even more smoke rising from it. I did not see any other ships, at least not to my left – because my vision was concentrated to that side – except for the carrier.

Analysis

Ever since this attack was undertaken, the British have been insistent that all the Argentine reports about an attack on HMS *Invincible* are wrong, and that the ship was neither attacked nor hit. The Argentines

Ureta's A-4C C-321, seen later during the war, already decorated with the glowing-red 'kill' marking commemorating the alleged attack on HMS *Invincible*.

The A-4C C-318 or 321 at San Julián, a few days after the mission against HMS *Invincible*.

Ureta and Isaac after returning to San Julián following
the claimed attack on HMS *Invincible*.

remain persistent with their claims until this very day: unsurprisingly, related discussions are often heated.

What is certain is that the six fighter-bombers involved took off at 12:30; the Super Etendards fired their Exocet two hours later, and then returned to land at 15:30. The two surviving Skyhawks landed back at the base at 16:23. At 15:40, the BAM Malvinas forwarded a message from the FAA's radar on the Falklands to CdoFAS:

> … lots of British helicopters were detected over the fleet, all moving to the east, where the HMS *Invincible* was supposed to be, and the Sea Harriers – which flew their CAPs at an altitude of 30,000ft – were landing at a different point than the one where they have taken off.[3]

The rest of the Argentine version of this affair is based on what Ureta and Isaac claim to have seen: both of them agreed that the ship they bombed was the same that they saw in the pictures before the mission, that it had a rectangular flight deck, a big long island, and the two radar masts. They also both stressed that they had left that ship enveloped in a dense cloud of black smoke, rising from about the centre of the hull, below the island. Moreover, the two Super Etendard pilots stated that the target that they had tracked with their radars was the size of an aircraft carrier.

Once the corresponding reports were published in Argentina, late on 30 May, the British Defence Minister John Nott stated that the Argentines had re-attacked the burned-out hulk of SS *Atlantic Conveyor*, and that one Skyhawk was shot down. Actually, *Atlantic Conveyor* had sunk already two days earlier, which means that Nott's statement was false. Three days later, the British stated that the Skyhawks actually attacked the Type 21 frigate HMS *Avenger* (F185), which – together with the destroyer HMS *Exeter* (D89) – was south-east of the Royal Navy's task force and heading for the islands with the task of providing fire-support the following night. The frigate was seven miles south-west of the

The flight sheet of the 30 May mission of Gerardo Isaac.

destroyer, and 24 miles west of HMS *Invincible* at the time of attack: about 45 seconds after the incoming airstrike was detected it may have shot down the approaching Exocet with her 4.5in (115mm) gun. The two Skyhawks were then shot down by Sea Dart SAMs fired by HMS *Exeter*, and the black smoke seen by the Argentine pilots was 'normal' for such a ship. With their own navy operating exactly the same guns on its two British-made destroyers, the Argentines concluded this version as 'very doubtful', because they consider such guns as ineffective for use even against aircraft, not to mention sea-skimming missiles.

Whether they actually attacked the British aircraft carrier, or a frigate, there is little doubt that the Skyhawks managed to penetrate the defences of the Royal Navy's task force and their pilots demonstrated bravery beyond what could have been expected from them. Unsurprisingly, Isaac

A view at the long island of HMS *Invincible* during an underway-replenishing operation from RFA *Fort Grange*, on 2 June 1982. Note that this photograph shows no evidence of damage to *Invincible*. (Photo by John-Charles Osmond)

and Ureta were both decorated with the Medalla al Heroico Valore n Combat – the highest military award of Argentina.[4]

8
A DOUBLE TRAGEDY

Following the attack on 30 May 1982, the entire Grupo 4 of IV Brigada Aérea was left with only seven operational A-4Cs. Unsurprisingly, CdoFAS de-facto ordered Escuadrón I Aeromóvil to stand down. Escuadrón II Aeromóvil remained on stand-by, but because of the bad weather and the difficulties with finding targets, largely because there were no more observers close to San Carlos Bay or in other zones where the Royal Navy operated, no combat sorties took place on the following days. This changed on 5 June, when CdoFAS issued OF.1281, that ordered Puño Flight – including PT Berrier (C-221), TT Omar Gelardi (C-226), PT Danilo Bolzán (C-214), and TT Cervera (C-228) to fly armed reconnaissance over Queen Charlotte Bay /Bahía San Julián, to the southwest of West Falkland/Gran Malvina. Armed with three BRP.250s each, the aircraft reached the designated target zone, but found nothing and returned safely at 16:10. The FAA thus remained unable to influence the progress of the fighting on the ground, and the British advance on Port Stanley progressed largely undisturbed.

Fateful Decisions
On 6 June CdoFAS received a report from 5th Battalion of the Marine Infantry (Batallón de Infanteria de Marina 5, BIM 5) about the appearance of RFA *Sir Tristram* off Fitzroy Settlement, in Pleasant Bay, and the landing of 2 PARA of the British Army. The British had secured a bridgehead but, concerned about the threat of land-based Exocets – which they knew the Argentine Navy had meanwhile deployed on the islands – the Royal Navy then launched another landing at Bluff Cove.

A-4B (C-239) and a row of A-4Cs ready for a mission at San Julián, during the last few days of the war.

A view into one of the hardened aircraft shelters at San Julián, with an A-4C undergoing maintenance inside.

The amphibious assault ships HMS *Fearless* and HMS *Intrepid* moved in that direction along a route north of Lively Island: the related reports were exactly what CdoFAS had waited for for over a week: late on 8 June 1982, Brigadier-General Crespo ordered Escuadrón II Aeromóvil to launch an attack. Potro Flight – including PT Bolzán (C-204), Vicecomodoro Ernesto Dubourg (C-207), and PT Héctor Sánchez (C-240), each armed with three BRP.250s – were airborne by 08:30. Sánchez recalled:

We took off very early, before the dawn and reached the islands at sunrise. Bolzán was flying ahead and when we reached the coast of Gran Malvina, an immense flock of birds started flying ahead of us, millions of birds. I had them in front of my aircraft and tried to avoid them, I thought we will not survive. When we returned I saw that one of the birds hit the nose of a bomb on Dubourg's aircraft, damaging the fuse, while another destroyed the beacon below my aircraft. Because we didn't find the target, we returned and remained on alert until the next day.

Meanwhile, at 9:30 Trueno Flight departed under OF.1282, with Captain Carlos Varela (C-212), TTs Roca (C-230) and Sergio Mayor (C-214), and Alférez Moroni (C-228). Their task was to attack British ground forces concentrated on Mount Kent. Moroni recalled:

On June 7, a mission was planned where we were going with four aircraft to bomb from high altitude with six bombs each. We were going to pass in [a] formation and height on the orders of the radar. That day […] a Learjet that acted as pathfinder for many other attack formations was shot down, and thus the ground control ordered us to abort and return. Each of our aircraft had a single MER

A-4B C-214: the Skyhawk flown by PT Bolzán on an armed reconnaissance over Queen Charlotte Bay on 5 June and then by TT Sergio Mayor an attack on Mount Kent on 8 June 1982.

Rows of A-4Cs (left and top) and A-4Bs at BAM San Julián late during the war.

The landing support ship RFA *Sir Galahad* as seen before the war.

RFA *Sir Tristram* (foreground), RFA *Sir Lancelot* (centre, left) and HMS *Fearless* (background) seen at Ascension Island in April 1982. (Photo by Bob Shackleton)

A-4B serial C-212 was flown by Capitán Carlos Varela, a member of Trueno Flight on 8 June 1982. This photograph shows it a few days later.

I was a qualified flight-leader, but never did this in combat before. Now, and suddenly, I was in command, and then of not one, but of two flights. I remember Captain Carballo saying "attack with a difference of one minute, three ahead and two behind... and take them to Glory!" I felt a shiver, but then I felt reassured, as all the men with me were prepared for this kind of mission and the success of the operation depended on my leading.

Over Belgrano Cape (southern end of Gran Malvina/West Falkland) we flew over a zone of rain which lasted for some seconds. We crossed the southern end of the Sound. The sea was full of gulls flying calmly. The next waypoint was Aguila Island and there we crossed another zone of rain. From there we continued on a direct line to Fitzroy.

We crossed Bahía del Laberinto/Adventure Sound, where we had more rain for about 30 seconds (about 8 kilometres). I was about to return, fearing the rain was covering the whole islands, but we saw clarity behind the water curtain, so I followed our path.

Then we crossed Choiseul Sound and I ordered to accelerate to reach 900 km/h, while we flew closer to the sea. 40 seconds before the target we saw a Sea Lynx, so I hid behind some hills to avoid their detection.

Twenty seconds later we found a Sea King landed, we did the same evasion manoeuvre and arrived at Fitzroy; there was nothing there. I decided to fly thirty seconds to the north. We saw lots of British troops on the ground below us: they opened fire and a missile crossed behind us, from right to left, on a climb angle of about 30°.

When we were finishing our turn Gómez shouted "there are the ships!" Two grey silhouettes could be seen against the coast, "stop turning and turn to the left!" I attacked and released my bombs, hitting the centre of RFA *Sir Galahad*. Rinke's bombs bell behind the ship, hitting the ground and destroying a vehicle there. Carmona also scored hits. The pair behind us saw the mast of the ship passing slowly, and thus went after RFA *Sir Tristram*. Gálvez and Gómez didn't waste their bombs.

I escaped "looking for water" as we said in the flight. Then I checked if all of us were returning. We were. We inspected each

under the centreline, and we were actually six in formation, because of the reserve, Guillermo Dellepiane, flying with us.

Because half of the Welsh Guards were still aboard *Fearless*, the Royal Navy then decided to transfer them to RFA *Sir Galahad*, and this ship – together with RFA *Sir Tristram*, to bring them to Fitzroy during the night of 7 to 8 June. However, once in the zone, the Welsh Guards were informed that because the Argentines had destroyed the bridge between Bluff Cove and Fitzroy, they had to march longer than planned. Because of this, the commanders decided to keep their troops onboard the ships and wait for the landing craft to pick them up, so they could travel by sea instead of marching. The troops of BIM 5 saw the ships and reported their appearance, and thus CdoFAS ordered an attack by one flight of Daggers and two of A-4Bs. This is how Grupo 5 de Caza came to deliver what many in the British armed forces subsequently declared the 'darkest day of the fleet'.

Bluff Cove

The Dagger flight approached first, but due to a navigation error ended up attacking targets on the northern side of Falkland Sound/San Carlos Strait. Escuadrón II Aeromóvil's Skyhawks followed. Mastín Flight (OF.1289) including PT Filippini (C-250), TTS Gálvez (C-214) and Autiero (C-237), and Alférez Hugo Gómez (C-230), launched at 11:30. Behind them was Dogo Flight (OF.1290) with Captain Carballo (C-201), TT Rinke (C-221), PT Cachón (C-222) and Alférez Carmona (C-240). The leaders of both flights had to return as also did TT Autiero, so the first group was led to the Falklands/Malvinas by Lt Gálvez and the second by Cachón. The latter recalled:

A crewmember of RFA *Sir Lancelot* next to an Argentine BR.250 bomb lodged inside the ship.

RFA *Sir Galahad* afire after the attack by Dogo Flight on 8 June 1982 – which caused the 'black day' for the Royal Navy.

RFA *Sir Lancelot*, after being damaged by the A-4Cs.

The burned-out and still smouldering hulk of RFA *Sir Galahad*. The ship was eventually scuttled as a war grave.

other's aircraft: Gálvez and Gómez were hit. This day hurt the enemy very much, I accomplished what my chief had requested.

In fact, Carmona's bombs failed to release. Lieutenant-Colonel David Chaundler, commander of 2 PARA, was on the coast when the Skyhawks appeared:

Four Skyhawks came in at mast level, the hatch was open on the deck, and this thousand-pound bomb went straight in. All these Welsh Guardsmen appeared on deck. We were absolutely appalled, as we had no idea there were any troops on board.

Although four Sea Harries were on a CAP over the combat zone, they were all from the *Hermes*-embarked NAS.800, which flew its patrols at much too high an altitude. Thus, they failed to intervene, leaving the Skyhawks to return to their base unmolested. RFA *Sir Galahad* caught fire immediately and her skipper, Captain Roberts, ordered the crew to abandon ship. Thirty-five minutes after the attack, all the non-seriously injured personnel and crew had been evacuated and by this time, the whole of the bridge front was burning furiously. The badly wounded were evacuated from the forecastle by helicopter, completing the evacuation one hour after the attack. In total 43 Welsh Guards and seven ships' crew were killed.

Final Catastrophe

Encouraged by reports from returning pilots about the presence of Royal Navy ships at Bluff Cove, CdoFAS decided to exploit this success and destroy the British landing. Thus, two additional flights were scrambled. This was however an obvious mistake, because by then the British were on alert and the crucial moment of surprise was lost. OF.1296 ordered Mazo Flight – including PT Danilo Bolzán (C-204), Alférez Guillermo Dellepiane (C-239) and TT Juan Arrarás (C-226) – into action. This was followed by Martillo Flight (OF.1297), including PT Oscar Berrier (C-212), Alférez Alfredo Vázquez (C-228) and PT Héctor

A bomb hole low down on the stern of RFA *Sir Tristam*: this hit cause a fire within the cargo space, which subsequently spread into the superstructure.

The burned out stern and superstructure of RFA *Sir Tristam* seen while undergoing repairs with the help of MV *Rangatira* in Port Stanley after the war.

Sánchez (C-231). Each aircraft was armed with three BRPs, and they were airborne by 15:00. Martillo 1 then developed problems with its oxygen supply system and had to abort early, while Mazo 2 developed engine problems during the IFR-opration. Sánchez recalled:

When the first two flights were sent, we asked to go with them, but the command said we had to wait until their return. I had a bad feeling, because we were losing the surprise. After the first group returned, we were ordered to go, it was very late, after 14:00. My guide returned, the only one of my flight equipped with Omega. The weather was very bad and it was very hard for me to find the tanker, as without Omega I had to do it with the help of stopwatch and compass only. Finally, I saw the tanker, refuelled, and then waited for Bolzán, who had the Omega. Dellepiane returned and four of us continued to the target, I was No.3.

We approached from the south, very low and after passing San Carlos Strait we turned to Puerto Argentino, leaving Goose Green to our left. Before reaching the target zone, we had to check the fuel, and then I realised that one of my drop tanks wasn't transferring. Thus, I was already below the minimum required to return to the base.

Theoretically, I was supposed to abort but, we were now only five minutes from the target, and thus I decided to continue. We passed by Pleasant Bay and then saw columns of smoke and ships

on fire. We flew in parallel to the bay [slightly to the north of Fitzroy; author's note], we were over the ground, to the south of the mounts Kent and Harriet, going to the sea to look for more ships. The troops had landed and started to fire at us – missiles, 30mm, 20mm – from the other shore. The leader reached the initial point and pulled the throttle lever to the limit and I delayed in doing so, so Vázquez passed me. I pulled the throttle, they were firing from our right and then the infantry was in front of us and we saw a curtain of bullets. From higher up, I could see the people throwing themselves on the ground as we passed overhead. I armed my guns and pressed the trigger, but both jammed after only two rounds. Then I felt some impacts in my aircraft. We left the coast and headed southwest, following the coast. I continued at full throttle trying to reach Vázquez and return to my position in the formation. I don't know why, I looked to my rear and I saw the impact of 30mm shots on the water and I thought 'someone is firing against me'. From the coast I saw nothing, I thought that must be a ship from the sea, but I couldn't see anything. At the same moment I saw the three Skyhawks turning fast to the right and crossing my flight path in front of me. I was passing Vázquez, who turned to the island and I had to jink up, to avoid a collision. Then I saw the landing vessel, I climbed to almost 2,000 feet and I thought, "at this height someone will shoot me down."

I saw them attacking the *F4*, Bolzán got in and attacked: the

Landing Craft Utility (LCU) *F4* from HMS *Fearless*, sunk by the A-4Bs of Mozo Flight on 8 June 1982, with the loss of six crewmembers.

A-4B C-226 flown by TT Juan Arrarás as seen from a KC-130H tanker while refuelling on 8 June: about an hour later, this Skyhawk was shot down and its pilot killed by an AIM-9L Sidewinder launched by David Morgan from a Sea Harrier.

vessel was coming from Choiseul Sound from the west and we were coming from the east. Bolzán hit the vessel on the rear part and at least one bomb detonated. Arrarás hit the vessel in the middle, all his three bombs detonating. Vázquez got in on a bad position and flew over the bow, I don't know if he managed to drop the bombs. I was watching the action in front of me and preparing my attack, when something attracted my attention to the right and the same height: there they were, about 700 metres away, two Sea Harriers flown by David Morgan and David Smith. I saw the first missile fired by Morgan, an impressive contrail, so I shouted to my wingmen. I saw the missile going down, Bolzán turned to the left at very low height. Arrarás and Vázquez climbed in a manoeuvre to face the missile, reducing power, to reduce the heat from the engine. The aircraft reached the same height as me, the missile went down, then climbed and hit the tail of Arrarás, he ejected and when I saw his parachute opening I felt better, but he was falling into water and there was nobody to rescue him. Then I watched again the Sea Harriers and I saw another missile, I'm sure from Smith's plane. The missile flew low along the water surface, but this time arrived to almost the centre of Vázquez' aircraft before the proximity fuse activated. The aircraft exploded and converted into a ball of fire. I was shocked, you think "this was your friend," you cannot believe what you are seeing....

Until then I was only a spectator, I had nothing to fire against them. When I recovered from the shock, I watched again for the Sea Harriers but they were gone. Then I looked up and saw one of them above me, turning down to attack me. I jettisoned everything, the fuel tanks and the TER with the bombs and pressed the throttle fully forward. I went as close to the water as I could and headed for Choiseul Sound, looking into my mirror to see the contrail of a missile. I think Morgan went for Bolzán, as we never talked again. I was trying to find the aircraft that was attacking me, but he flew into the Sound ahead of me. It began to rain and there were low clouds ahead of me: I wanted to get there and hide: underway, I manoeuvred very hard to one side and the other to avoid an attack with guns. Finally, I reached the cloud and to the south of the Isla Soledad: from there, I flew straight back to Río Gallegos, always at very low height and looking to my back. Then I remembered my fuel problem, I was sweating, hysteric, it's hard to describe what happens in your head in such a situation.

When I passed San Carlos and lateral to Gran Malvina I continued flying low. I did not dare to climb. My fuel wasn't enough to reach Río Gallegos, so I started to climb to 20,000 feet. My options were to return to Puerto Argentino or to go to Río Gallegos and eject when the fuel was out. Puerto Argentino was very dangerous. Then I thought that maybe the tanker was still flying. I called them and they answered that they were still in the zone. I told them that we were four but I was returning alone and with no fuel. The pilot, Vicecomodoro Cano [the co-pilot was Captain Rubik; author's note], said, "don't worry lad" and he started giving me coordinates. I replied "my aircraft is standard," which meant that I didn't have Omega and because of my distance to the mainland I couldn't find VOR or ADF signals, I was on heading 270°. While climbing, the canopy started to blur, because one of the bullets that hit me had broken the air conditioning. The KC-130H, using my VHF signal, indicated a heading to me, so I turned to the right. I told them I had only 500 pounds of fuel: the manual dictated that if the amount was down to 200, it was unsafe to fly. They said they were heading to the islands and that I would see the Hercules in a few moments. I replied "I will not reach you! If I eject please advise, so someone could look for me." Meanwhile, an A-4C flight was going to the islands (Yunque Flight), one of them was Lt Paredi and when he told me he was going to Pleasant Bay, I alerted him that I was returning from there and that my three wingmen were shot down by Sea Harriers.

Then I saw a dot on the horizon and told the Hercules crew that

I think I have them in sight, so I asked them to turn to the right and head to Río Gallegos and I saw the dot turning to the right, I felt relieved, but I was still far from them. When I was approaching I watched the fuel indicator and I had only 200 pounds and I thought "Pipi, you're screwed." I continued without touching the throttle nor watching the fuel indicator. The Hercules had finished its turn and had the basket deployed. I was very fast and I only wanted to reach them to receive the fuel. When I was very close I realised I had an excess of speed, so I reduced throttle and passed them by their side and informed them "don't worry, I have too much speed and I will manoeuvre to approach again." When I passed them I went up and the shouted "look out!", I made a barrel and returned to my position and reached the basket on the first attempt. I refuelled and then returned to Río Gallegos at sunset [it was 18:00; author's note]. I landed and parked on the apron. My mechanic came to my plane, the others were seated on the blocks used to keep the aircraft immovable on the tarmac. I shut down the engine and opened the canopy. I felt very bad, I threw my helmet, I felt destroyed, it was very cold, I felt my body cold, my soul cold. I went to the pilot's room and cried a lot. Then Varela and Cervera came to ask me what happened. We learned that we didn't have to face the missiles, we only have to run as fast and low as we could if we were intercepted.

The flight had destroyed LCU *F4* from HMS *Fearless*, carrying vehicles from Goose Green to Fitzroy when they were intercepted by two Sea Harriers. David Morgan, a pilot of the Royal Air Force on an exchange tour with the Royal Navy, recalled that he saw the LCU underway from Goose Green and then, suddenly spotted a Skyhawk about a mile away, approaching at very low altitude:

I jammed the throttle fully open, shouted over the radio "A-4s attacking the boat. Follow me down!" and peeled off into a sixty-degree dive towards the attacker. As my airspeed rattled up through 400 knots I retracted my flaps and pushed to zero G to achieve the best possible rate of acceleration… I watched impotently, urging my aircraft onward and downward, as the A-4 opened fire with his 20-millimetre cannon, bracketing the tiny craft. My heart soared as his bomb exploded a good 100 feet beyond the landing craft but then sank as I realised that a further A-4 was running in behind him. The second pilot did not miss and I bore mute and frustrated witness to the violent fire-bright petals of the explosion, which obliterated the stern, killing the crew and mortally wounding the landing craft. All-consuming anger welled in my throat and I determined in that instant that this pilot was going to die!

As I closed rapidly on his tail I noticed in my peripheral vision a further A-4 skimming the spume-flecked water, paralleling his track to my left. I hauled my aircraft to the left and rolled out less than a half mile behind the third fighter, closing like a runaway train. I had both missiles and guns selected and within seconds I heard the growl in my earphones which told me that my Sidewinder could see the heat from his engine. My right thumb pressed the lock button on the stick and instantly the small green missile cross in the head-up display transformed itself into a diamond sitting squarely over the back end of the Skyhawk. At the same time the growl of the missile became an urgent high-pitched chirp, telling me that the infrared homing head of the weapon was locked on and ready to fire.

I raised the safety latch and mashed the recessed red firing button with all the strength I could muster. There was a short delay as the missile's thermal battery ignited. In less than half second the Sidewinder was transformed from an inert eleven-foot drainpipe

A close-up view of A-4B C-204, flown by PT Danilo Bolzán on 8 June 1982: this was the aircraft that sunk *F4* but was shot down by Sea Harriers – and its pilot killed – shortly afterwards.

The third A-4B pilot of V Brigada Aérea shot down and killed on 8 June 1982 was Alférez Vázquez. This photograph shows him (on the left) together with Captain Del Valle Palaver, shot down on 25 May.

into a fire-breathing monster as it accelerated to nearly three times the speed of sound and streaked towards the nearest enemy aircraft… Within two seconds the missile had disappeared directly up his jet pipe and what had been a vibrant flying machine was completely obliterated as the missile tore it apart. The pilot had no chance of survival.

There was no time for elation. As I was righting my machine after the first missile launch, I realised that I was pointing directly at another Argentine aircraft at a range of about a mile – the one I had seen hit the landing craft.

Unknown to me, on my entry into the fight I had mistaken the third Skyhawk for the rearmost man, a mistake that could have cost me my life. As I was about to line up my sights on the second A-4 the rear man was manoeuvring in an attempt to spoil my whole day with a stream of high explosive rounds. I had made the classic mistake of barrelling into the fight without total situational awareness. As a result I had nearly collided with the fourth Skyhawk and I was now directly in front of him."[1]

Morgan's recollection differs from that by Sánchez in the order of his firings as he says he first shot down Vázquez and then Arrarás. He also stated that he did not fire at Sánchez's aircraft, while the later states he saw splashes behind him – which would indicate a cannon attack by Morgan:

He obviously saw the Sidewinder launch because he immediately reversed his break and pulled his aircraft into a screaming turn away from it. This was without doubt the best possible evasive action he could have tried as it made the missile expend a huge amount of energy and control power to reverse its course. His best efforts were to no avail, however, and the thin grey missile flashed back across my nose and, seemingly in slow motion, pulled to the right and impacted his machine directly behind the cockpit. [2]

Morgan's wingman, Lieutenant Dave Smith recalled his involvement in this action:

Dave Morgan and I launched from HMS *Hermes* on the first of our "duskers" sorties to carry out a CAP south west of Stanley in the immediate overhead of HMS [actually RFA] *Galahad*. I think the transit was about 200 miles and the CAP was initially at 10,000 feet. *Galahad* had been hit by bombs earlier and I remember a thick cloud of black smoke pouring out of her and the aft end literally glowing red with the intensity of the fires below decks. We were right at the end of our time on task and about to depart back to *Hermes* when Dave spots four aircraft below. His actual words were something like "F..k me Dave! Four mirages! Follow me down!" (Subsequently turned out to be A-4's). We were 180 degrees out in a turn at the time and he promptly disappeared from sight into the gathering gloom. I rolled and pulled and went for the deck at full power calling Dave for the attack heading. He came back with something like "240" and I pulled out at about 150 feet doing just over 600 knots heading south west. I still couldn't see anything but a few seconds later Dave opened up in quick succession with both his Sidewinders. I saw these missiles hit the back two A-4s and thereby got visual with Dave. One of the A-4 pilots had ejected and I very nearly picked him up on my wing in his parachute! Dave was then closing the third A-4 and opened up with his cannons. From the bullet splashes on the water I finally got a 'tally' on the target and as Dave pulled off and out of the picture. I got a good IR lock from one of my AIM-9Ls. I reckoned I was at about 50 feet at this stage still doing about 615 knots and I still couldn't put the A-4 on the horizon so he must have been quite low. The range looked a bit excessive and I remember hesitating for a second or two trying to assess whether it was worth taking the shot. At that very moment Sharkey Ward comes on the radio and says "OK, we are coming in from the south and taking over!" or words to that effect. This caused me to completely loose the bubble! Although I had seen Dave shoot at this target I hadn't positively identified it and I had an instant of pure panic as I questioned if it was actually Sharkey or Steve Thomas I had in my sights. Well, I fired anyway and this prompted "Who fired that shot?" from Sharkey and for a ghastly moment I thought I had shot at Steve. Then Steve came back with "It wasn't

me, Boss" and I heaved a sigh of relief. The missile tracked the A-4 and then seemed to flame out. I was fairly certain it wouldn't hit but then at the very end of its trajectory it detonated and destroyed the target.

Eventually, Arrarás ejected, but he was never recovered. Morgan fired his 30mm guns at Bolzán's aircraft but missed due to a failure of his HUD. He climbed and left Smith to attack Bolzán instead. Sánchez returned to base at 18:00.

Frustrating Experiences

On the morning of 8 June 1982, CdoFAS issued an order for Escuadrón II Aeromóvil to re-deploy to BAM San Julián, while the Daggers on that base switched to Río Gallegos: with this, all of the FAA's A-4s would operate from San Julián. Moroni recalled:

We made that transfer during the night of 8 June: the first two were Teniente Mayor and me. I was about to start when I saw Pipi returning alone from his mission. …We arrived at San Julián at night, knowing that there were three aircraft that had not returned. The rest of both the A-4B and A-4C squadrons followed the next day: they flew attack sorties before returning to San Julián but found no targets.

Indeed, CdoFAS exploited the opportunity offered by the re-deployment of Escuadrón II Aeromóvil, to task it with additional airstrikes on targets in the Bluff Cove area. OF.1302 launched Pitón Flight from Río Gallegos on 8 June 1982 at 14:00. This included A-4Bs flown by PT Berrier (C-212), Alférez Dellepiane (C-230) and TT Gelardi (C-227) and was supposed to attack together with Cobra Flight from 4 Grupo de Caza, but the latter missed the route and flew away towards the north. Pitón Flight thus reached Bluff Cove alone, but found no targets, and returned to San Julián at 17:15.

Shortly after, even the Escuadrón I Aeromóvil was ordered into action again: Yunque flight of A-4Cs launched at 15:36 under OF.1298. This formation included Capitán Caffarati (C-322), TTs Záttara (C-321) and Paredi (C-318), and Alférez Codrington (C-324). Guided by the VLF Omega nav/attack system of Caffarati's C-322, the flight descended about 100 miles short of the islands and reached the combat zone unmolested. At five miles to the target they saw RFA *Sir Galahad* (L3005) still on fire and turned to bomb the British troops on the beach: Number 1 dropped only two bombs, while numbers 3 and 4 could not release even a single one. All pilots recalled encountering intensive anti-aircraft fire, and according to Cordington (Number 4),

Damage caused by an Albatross strike on C-314 on 9 June 1982 when it was piloted by Alférez Guillermo Martínez, which forced him to abandon the mission and return to the mainland.

During the final days of the war, A-4Q 3-A-309 received this test paint scheme, consisting of grey, with a mottled pattern of brown and olive green.

at least six SAMs, two of which Paredi saw exploding near the exhaust pipes of Caffarati's and Záttara's aircraft, while another exploded behind his Skyhawk. On the flight back to Argentina, the formation saw a pair of Sea Harriers on a CAP station high above them, but passed below them unobserved: all aircraft returned safely, even if C-318 and C-321 were damaged and leaking fuel, and the KC-130H had to 'tow' them until they were close to the runway.

Also active over the Islas Malvinas that day were the A-4Qs of 3° Escuadrilla, COAN: TN Oliveira (3-A-301) and TF Olmedo (3-A-305) were ordered to attack a suspected British helicopter base on Broken Island. Both Skyhawks reached the target zone unmolested but found no helicopters and instead released five Mk.82 bombs each upon the local buildings.

On 9 June 1982, CdoFAS planned another attack against the bridgehead at Fitzroy. Correspondingly, OF.1303 ordered Cobra Flight to launch at 14:00, with Captain Almoño (C-302), PT Costantino (C-312) and Alferez Guillermo Martínez (C-314) and Isaac (C-322). Constantino was forced to abort shortly after taking off, and Isaac shortly after refuelling from the KC-130H, but the other two continued the mission. Due to a navigation mistake, Almoño and Martínez arrived 20 miles due north of their intended target and had to follow the coast all the way to Fitzroy. About a minute before reaching the target, Martínez's Skyhawk collided with a bird, which caused a fuel leak and damaged his brakes. Eventually, both pilots returned to base having failed to find any targets. C-314 had to use its hook to stop with the help of the arrestor wire at the end of the runway.

After this action, due to a lack of intelligence about suitable targets and limited operational aircraft, IV Brigada Aérea's A-4Cs were de-facto grounded and did not fly for the rest of the war. Indeed, not only C-314, but also C-318 and C-324 were out of service due to combat damage, while C-312 and C-321 were unserviceable for other reasons. Thus, Escuadrón I Aeromóvil was down to only two A-4Cs – C-302 and C-322 – in fully mission capable condition.

The condition of the A-4Qs of 3° Escuadrilla was quite similar. Nevertheless, the unit continued flying: TN Rótolo and TC Médici took off in 3-A-301 and 3-A-302 respectively, to attack the British landing ships damaged the day before at Bluff Cove. After refuelling from the KC-130H and when they were only 19 minutes from the target, the Beech B-200 4-G-44 that acted as radio relay cancelled the

mission because of the presence of three pairs of Sea Harriers over the target zone.

Frustrated, the Argentine naval pilots thus concentrated on their secondary tasks during the following days: a training flight was undertaken on 10 June by TN Benitez in 3-A-302, and a post-repair test-flight by TN Sylvester – the latter to check the 3-A-306 damaged in Zubizarreta's ejection.

Last-Ditch Attempts

Escuadrón II Aeromóvil's A-4Bs were still operational, and on 12 June CdoFAS ordered them into action with OF.1312: this directed Alfa Flight – including Capitán Bergamaschi (C-207), Alférez Barrionuevo (C-236), and TTs Fernando Robledo (C-230) and Ossés (C-224) – to bomb British artillery positions at Port Harriet House with three BRP.250s each. By this time, the A-4Bs were all clearly showing their age: Numbers 1 and 4 were both forced to abort after the IFR-operation, while the Number 3 developed problems after reaching the islands alone, and thus returned to base without attacking. The second flight was Paris (OF.1314), the task of which was an anti-ship attack in San Carlos. It launched at 15:20 and was led by Capitán Carballo in C-221. However, while taking-off, TT Rinke's Skyhawk caught fire, forcing the pilot to abort: the aircraft was brought to a stop with the help of the arresting wire at the end of the runway. Because of this, the take-off of TT Gálvez and Alférez Gómez was cancelled and Carballo continued alone to perform a reconnaissance close to the islands. He saw a ship without a flag and crew and requested permission from the CIC to attack her but authorization was denied. At 17:00 he landed at San Julián.

3° Escuadrilla also flew its last mission of the war on this day: TN Rótolo launched in 3-A-301 and TN Médici in 3-A-302. The two A-4Qs refuelled from a KC-130H and almost reached their target – British artillery positions north of North Basin – before they sighted a pair of Sea Harriers. Both pilots promptly jettisoned their bombs and returned to Río Grande. Grupo 5 de Caza flew its final sorties of the war on 13 June. Nene Flight included Capitán Zelaya (C-230), TTs Gelardi (C-227) and Cervera (C-212) and Alférez Dellepiane (C-221), while Chispa Flight (OF.1320) included Capitán Varela (C-222), TTs Roca (C-250) and Mayor (C-235), and Alférez Moroni (C-237). All aircraft were armed with three BRP.250s each. Zelaya had to return

Armed with three 250kg BR bombs each, these A-4B Skyhawks of Escuadrón II Aeromóvil were photographed while ready for the next combat sortie, during the last few days of the war.

Taken on the same occasion, this photograph shows A-4B serial C-222, painted grey overall and nick-named El Tordillo (see colour section for further details).

and running troops, so that's where I aimed my bombs.

During the egress I encountered a Sea King helicopter flying perpendicular to me, from right to left. I had the sight collimated for 260 mils – for low-level bombing – so I started to shoot my guns by eyesight, seeing the streak of tracers converging into the big helicopter. I came dangerously close to the Sea King and could clearly see the light blue helmets of the pilots, and then I pulled up and passed over it.

After this manoeuvre, and when I had levelled my Skyhawk, I heard Dellepiane desperately calling, "Tucu, break right! Break right!" I did this immediately, banking 90 hard to the side, while pulling as tight as possible, and jettisoning all external stores. Simultaneously, I saw a pair of missiles with a bright flame on their rear end pass very close to my left side, fast as hell. While in my panic turn, and after releasing the stores, the A-4 skidded down so that only a few feet separated the hard ground from my right wingtip. In such a situation I had no alternative but to level my wings, relaxing the turn and gaining some space to make a better getaway.

Cervera escaped by flying at very low level. Dellepiane had the worst part of this mission, as he recalled:

June 13 was a very cold day, it was all snowy, we had gone to the base at San Julián and we were half lying on the mats because at night we did not sleep. This mission order came, we started to prepare things and went to the aircraft, I went to the aircraft that was at the head of the runway and because it was very cold I started the engines and the pipes of the hydraulic fluid burst, the mechanic told me that it was normal. One of the maintenance managers came, a reserve aircraft was always kept in case one failed, normally they were reserved for the squadron or section commanders. They gave me the other plane, it was close to the control tower, they took me, I went fast, I arrived, I got on, they started tying me, the other aircraft left. It was cloudy, an ugly day, I worried about preparing everything quickly, I was trying to leave when the chief of mechanics appeared and stopped me, I wanted to leave so fast that I had not set the aircraft to take off, so I adjusted the flaps, [and] the compensators and left.

When I went out, I did not see the others, I had made the take off so fast that I hadn't started the Omega, you have to start it on the ground. I left without that, I took off, I found the Hercules, I arrived, they were already finishing the refuelling, there I went directly to the refuelling and to the escadrille. One of the aircraft got fuel in the engine, that of Zelaya, who had to return. I was with Cervera

when fuel entered his engine during the IFR-operation. Nene Flight continued under Cervera's leadership, but then Varela announced that he would lead both flights because of his rank. Cervera recalled:

We arrived to the northwest of West Falkland/Gran Malvina. Flying over land by then, we heard our radar controller at Port Stanley calling "is anybody flying?" to which both flight leaders replied, giving course and details about the target we intended to attack. The controller gave us valuable information concerning the location of Sea Harrier CAPs. One was flying over Fitzroy, and the other two over the northern and southern end of Falkland Sound/San Carlos Strait, so we learned that we were restricted in our possible escape routes after the attack. Studying the situation, I suggested to captain Varela that perhaps it would be a good idea to return using the same route that we were following now, knowing that this was not covered by the deadly Sea Harriers. Although it was risky making a 180° turn under the enemies' noses, it was less dangerous than meeting a CAP. We were very near the target and it was harder to follow Chispas because heading changes occurred frequently and we lost sight of them sometimes in the rolling terrain. With my attention fully fixed on not losing them, I was quite surprised when I heard Captain Varela call "bombs away, go!", and then I saw the explosions of the 12 bombs.

During the attack I started to fire the Colt Mk 12 cannon as a defensive measure to keep heads down. Near the target I could not see very well due to the smoke and dirt produced by the preceding bombs, but when overflying it I saw four or five helicopters destroyed and people running in every direction. I did not drop the bombs because I thought I could find an intact target. After getting clear of the smoke and confusion, I saw more helicopters and Gelardi and the escadrille that was behind us went to lead the formation, which was that of Varela.

It rained at some moments and to the north of the islands we were heading east, there were times when we followed the aircraft ahead because the wake was marked in the water, because we were very low, about 5 meters. Then, when we arrived north of the islands, we headed south. Five minutes before the attack, the radar at Puerto Argentino came on asking if there was any airplane in the area and Varela tells them that we were there. They began to pass the location of the CAPs, which were one to the east of Puerto Argentino, another to the west, several to the south and one to the north of the San Carlos Strait. We had planned to attack and continue to the south but we said 'no, we attack and return to the north', because the worst was in the south.

The first escadrille attacked, then we did it ourselves, it was two squares of containers and tents, we dropped the 500-pound bombs. We had Varela's flight ahead, but you concentrate on your aircraft and do not look at it. We dropped the bombs and got out. Cervera came out, they threw him a missile, I tell him to change the turn, the missile explodes on a hill, I continued straight and there I see a helicopter, I shot at it, it was on a hill, 4 or 5 shots went out and the guns were locked, but I hit him on a blade and [he] landed in an emergency. I then left to the right, I already had dropped the bombs and I saw another helicopter to the north, that was landed.

There is something in the procedures in the A-4 that is forbidden and is to try to rearm the guns. When I saw it I rearmed them, I aimed, I shot and nothing came out, I passed very low, that's why I remember the colour of the pilot's helmet and then I left to the north.

The first thing we always did when we went out was to check the fuel, there I checked and had less than half of what I needed to have. So, they had hit me, when we made the attack, they were shooting from all sides. I pulled the handle to eject the tanks and I continued flying, it was very low. I went to the north and then to the west over the sea, I remember there was a ship. I wasn't going at full speed because of the fuel and I thought they were going to fire upon me, but they didn't. I didn't pass close, but I saw it well.

To the north of San Carlos Strait, I began to climb and I started to call the Malvinas radar to advise me about the Royal Navy's

Another photograph of the same line of A-4Bs, completing a left- and right-hand view of their camouflage and markings.

Alférez Barrionuevo pointing to the kill markings applied on his A-4B.

CAPs, because there was one north of the strait and I wanted to assure myself, but they told me that they didn't have that CAP on their radar any more. I asked the radar to ask the tanker to come to look for me, I had very little fuel, I would have had a thousand pounds, almost nothing. My main question was what to do, try to reach the mainland or eject. In the apprehension of leaving the aircraft I chose to continue. I had climbed high enough, reaching 38,000ft and remained there. Then I learned that there was one of the Hercules heading to get me.

Every time I looked around my big question was what to do: I was still worried about the Harriers and thus all the time looking around me. Then I stopped and continued. The fuel dropped to 500lbs, but the Hercules-crew told me not to worry. Finally, they said "we had you in sight", and to "turn to the right". However, this turned out to be another aircraft. Before that, when I was still over the islands, everyone wanted to give me advice, until Varela said to let me, that I knew what to do. When from the Hercules they said "it's not you" my heart dropped on the floor. Seconds passed… it is difficult to measure the time…then they said "we have you in sight", and then I saw them, low and to my right. The Hercules was down at 25,000ft, I was still at 38,000ft. They started to change

A-4B C-221, flown by Alférez Dellepiane seen while returning to the base while losing fuel after his mission on 13 June.

A-4B serial C-250 seen at San Julián on 13 June 1982, one day before the end of the war. (Photo by Hector Tessio)

you decide if you will go": the crew willingly risked its life to save me.

Chispa Flight had bombed the command post of Major General Sir Jeremy Moore and Brigadier Julian Thompson, commanders of the British ground forces, narrowly missing it. Their attack on a lonesome Sea King dented one of its main rotor blades. Moroni, who was with Nene Flight, recalled:

We made a navigation out of San Julián, we went a little to the northeast, we found the two tankers, we took fuel, we descended to low flight and the entrance to the islands was from north to south. We entered on Soledad Island and we all saw a helicopter that was stationary, we must have been about 1,500 meters or so away when he saw us. It had something white on the side, I do not know if it was a missile, I looked at the helicopter for a long time. A few seconds before seeing it the radar at BAM Malvinas calls us on frequency and asks if there was someone around, and the flight leader told him who we were. Varela's first question was if he had us in sight and he did not, so we were more calm. Next, the ground controller began to describe the British CAPs that were returning to their aircraft carriers, but later they returned to the islands and came to meet us. Luckily we maintained speed during our escape and they could not reach us. At a time when the radar had us in sight we had the CAP only 11 miles away, but we were able to maintain the speed advantage. When we attacked, something exploded between Varela and Mayor, we do not know if it was a missile, but it affected Varela's engine. Fortunately, he returned to San Julián even with reduced thrust.

I saw tents, vehicles and "vegetation" – which was anti-aircraft artillery. We went with three bombs [on] each aircraft and released from very low. Cervera, who was behind us, saw the impacts of the bombs and was oriented with that, and when he passed the infantry was firing with everything back at him. All the aircraft in our flight returned with multiple bullet holes: the worst was one in the right wing of Dellepiane's aircraft, causing him to lose fuel.

Roca commented:

The experience was very particular because it was the end of the war. We knew that the troops were close to Puerto Argentino, we knew that these missions had an added value for the course of the war, one way or the other. We knew it was a major concentration of troops, but not that it was the command post. We left almost at noon; the attack was at approximately 15:00. As for the weaponry, this consisted of three BRP.250s, with electric CAPA E fuses: it was

course, they came to the east and I was going to the west. When I went toward them I looked at my fuel and it was zero, I reduced the power of the engine and pulled down to reach them, I wasn't reaching them until I put more power. There is a distance at which it is difficult to appreciate the approach speed between two aircraft, until you realise that you're going to hit it: that's what happened to me. The aircraft accelerated a lot, I was not checking the speed indicator, I see the Hercules coming on me, so I told the pilot to dive the aircraft and add more power. I opened the air brakes, reduced power, I caught the hose, they were already ready to send the fuel, so the fuel started to pass. The tanker Hercules has a large window, I saw them jumping for joy, after so much tension I relaxed a lot until I loaded some fuel and I let go. Then they said, "negative, you're losing fuel from the drop tanks." I asked which ones, but then decided to jettison both. I looked back, but they didn't separate: thus, I attempted to jettison them again, until I realised I was losing fuel from the wing too. Thus, I remained connected to the basket until approaching the base, all the time losing as much fuel a I was receiving.

Because of the Hercules' slow speed – only 230 knots – it was a very long flight back home. When they left me on finals, I lowered the landing gear, but then the nosewheel refused to lower. I added power and used the emergency system to lower the gear. The Hercules followed, checking my landing gear until I landed. The KC-130 landed right after: they had no fuel left on board.

My Skyhawk received hits on the wing and later we found out that a Sea Harrier had chased the Hercules. The tanker was staying halfway between the Malvinas and the continent. When they were told about me, as it was so risky, they were told, "we don't order it, the first time that I was going to drop that type of fuse. Its arming was adjustable, its time of explosion also, which was what we should have had from the start. This bomb was the culmination of everything we had learned in those 70 days. The previous day we knew how the mission was prepared for that day. The only change was the problem in the refuelling with Zelaya's aircraft: he ingested fuel and had to return. Then Cervera continued with Dellepiane and Gelardi, which was his first combat mission. They slid back and let us lead, with Varela, me as second, Mayor as third, and Moroni as fourth.

It was an incredible day: the tankers TC-69 and 70 took us far north and far from the range of the radars. It was the first time I saw the two tankers together. It was a luxury because you left one and then you refuelled with the other. At the time we already had very few original drop tanks for the A-4Bs and Cs left because so many were jettisoned: the ones we had were those that had been built at Pescarmona Metallurgical Industries. The only difference was that they had an electrical probe that sent a signal about the consumption to the cockpit. We had a trick, which was to take-off with the pressurisation of the tanks disconnected, so that we would consume only the fuel from the internal tanks, thus making as if we did not have any extra tanks. Then we would connect the pressurisation and quickly filled the wing tanks to find out if the system was working – or not.

During in-flight refuelling operations, we always first filled the wing tank through the fuselage one, because that was faster. Drop tanks were kept filled all the time, so we were actually filling the wing and the fuselage tank.

We completed our refuelling operation and started the descent far out over the sea, as the goal was to enter from the north: our point of entry was San Luis. The planned exit point was in the south, but on the way back we went straight to the mainland.

What I remember is that we came very low over the sea and Varela broke the radio silence when we were already there, which was when he saw a helicopter, I did not see it, and the British did not see us. The ground control in Puerto Argentino advised us about enemy CAPs, enabling us to avoid these.

I remember that I was formed to the right of Varela. During the turn, I saw Puerto Argentino and I remember that we saw the top of the hills over us, then we entered fast between the rocks. The sun was low, it had snowed, there was nothing to interfere, mist or water vapor, it was an ideal day for an attack. That's when Varela sees this guy who was among the rocks, decides to fire and is when the mess started all simultaneously. Varela said "there they are, drop the bombs" or something like that. I was stuck, I was his wingman, I drop the bombs, the one that saw them was Cervera.

When the shooting started, I think it was Varela who said "we escape to the north" and Gelardi replied "where is the north?" In the middle of that madness, a guy with common sense asked that!

The bombs went out and I saw something that exploded near Varela and I saw pieces of something, I understand that they were from the tanks, some of the missiles that came out hit the tanks, not the plane. Then I remember that Mayor's aircraft was missing all the inspection covers. At the exit I did not see the helicopters until I left. Cervera saw the helicopters, he saw that we skipped them. Quite ahead in the escape I saw two helicopters, I remember that one dropped a bag that it had hanging down, I do not remember what it had, it was like a net and fell into the water, it must have been one or two minutes after the departure of the target. The only communications were when Dellepiane began to speak with Cervera and Varela, as he was losing fuel. I passed those helicopters,

Ricardo Lucero and Mariano Velasco being evacuated to the mainland on one of the Helicópteros Marinos' S-61 helicopters, after traveling from the islands on the ARA *Bahía Paraíso* hospital ship. (Photo by Oscar Arredondo)

Captain Pablo Carballo, the most successful flight leader of the FAA during the Malvinas War, with his personalised helmet, inside the cockpit of an A-4B.

Captain Pablo Carballo (left) and 1st Lt Alejandro Botana (who soloed on the A-4B shortly after the war).

I had never seen them so big and so close, I pass above one and the other by the side. The one I passed over was the one who dropped the bag, it gave me the idea that he was flying high but in fact was almost leaning on the water. After some 7 minutes and to the left there was a huge ship, a transport. I did not know where it was, nothing that I remember, but I said to myself "I got into San Carlos." I learned a few days later that San Carlos was to the left. I was only [armed] with the A-4's guns, with zero reliability. I went out to the north, in radio silence and I came across an aircraft that was Varela's, I overtook it, I was the first to land, it meant that I had

C-318 and 321 being prepared for a mission at BAM San Julián during June 1982.

passed the others.

I ejected the tanks and I realised when I landed that only one had come off, I never found out because I never looked outside. I ejected the loads and I felt the kick of the ejector foot that comes out, I heard the noise. It was the noise of the TER and the tanks. Actually, I returned with one and I exceeded the speed for the tank, so I crumpled it. An aircraft without tanks climbs to 45,000 feet with little fuel. I went up with everything because the tank had no fuel. In the descent, the fuel emergency light came on. I lowered the landing gear at 10,000 feet, I approached to reach the head of the runway at San Julián and I lowered the flaps at 8,000 feet, I had climbed to 47,000 feet, because I said "if the engine stops, the higher I am the closer I get." The engine stopped when I touched the runway, I got to the other end of the runway with the engine stopped and there I left the plane, I got off using the refuelling probe, I sat on the nose wheel, I lit a cigarette and when I turned around I realised that there was something left over, it was the tank, a mechanic who was coming said to me: "boss look at the tank." It was crumpled.

After me arrived Varela with reduced power, then Mayor, Moroni and Cervera. Most went to the tarmac and there was one that I do not remember who it was that went to the end, I think it was Varela.

According to Rick Strange, a Blowpipe operator who was part of the defence of the Brigade Headquarters at Mount Kent, the were three missile teams, each consisting of the Commander, Operator and Radio man.

We were laid out in a linear ambush position, I thought the position I had would be ideal in event of attack, we were worried about the amount of radio traffic and the detection by enemy direction-finding equipment. I can't recall the time of the attack. We had been static during the daylight hours, just watching our arcs and trying to stay warm, winter was starting to bite. I asked my Commander if it's ok to go and catch up with a friend whose missile team were the closest to Mt. Kent.

Literally seconds after I arrived, I said to my friend Cpl Pete Scotland "aircraft!" and indicated with a chopping hand the seven Skyhawk bombers approaching at a leisurely pace. My friend said "good one" but as he saw his two missile operators running away the penny dropped that was true. It was not my place to take command of his Blowpipe missile: I quickly readied the reload. Pete stood with the missile and I stood to his left, to spot. The missile was away after a slight hesitation, the distance was close but acceptable.

The missile missed the aircraft he was aiming at, I immediately ordered the destruction of the missile by shouting system switch.

By closing the switch this causes a self-destruct, I saw the lead aircraft venting fuel, struck by shrapnel, I shouted "a hit!" The bombs were away straight away, I saw the others in the group drop their bombs, I believe about five went off, a lot were on parachute drogue nets and these were still visible on the surface 20 years after the fighting finished.

I believe that a Gazelle helicopter and Scout received minor damage and a couple of Headquarter tents got slightly tattered. I've read a few accounts of that raid on how much anti-aircraft fire was put up. In truth there were only the three missile teams. The Headquarters was defended by about 30 men of Defence Section, these had light small arms and machine guns.

According to Strange, his team fired a missile towards Mount Estancia, while an explosion close to the other team impeded their fire. The missile fired by Pete Scotland most probably is the one that exploded between Varela and Mayor, causing damage to both aircraft. The other missile fired, according to him, did not engage any of the aircraft but hit a mountain: this was probably the round seen by Dellepiane while passing close to Cervera's Skyhawk. Strange concluded:

It was a quick action, over in seconds. I can't recall anyone claiming to have hit Dellepiane's aircraft. I knew the lads from the Defence Section, they would of [sic] crowed the loudest if they had a hit. Within minutes of the attack a Harrier came through chasing the raid. He was foolish to be on the same fly line as the raid. He had a healthy response from every one with a weapon. I was running around telling everyone to check fire as its friendly.

According to the accounts and the size of hole in Dellepiane's aircraft, the damage was not caused by a missile or small arms fire, but the shrapnel of one of his bombs. Nene Flight dropped their bombs on several Westland Sea King helicopters and later they damaged one Westland Scout and two Aerospatiale Gazelle helicopters. Although pursued by four Sea Harriers, they came away because British pilots failed to find them. Capitán Varela returned in his aircraft, C-222, with serious engine problems and other failures: he nearly ejected over the islands before deciding to return and managing to reach the mainland.

Conclusions

With the war ending on the morning of 14 June 1982, the top ranks of the FAA and CdoFAS, and surviving pilots received an opportunity to review their operations and results, while ground crews had the time to repair damaged and malfunctioning aircraft. One of the biggest issues related to the latter task was that of patching up the holes caused by the British small-arms-fire. For this purpose, the technicians consulted several car mechanics in Río Gallegos, who had a welder that provided help. However, the fuel gases inside the tanks made this task impossible. Ultimately, a Japanese dry cleaner provided help by using the vapour system from his shop to fill tanks with combustion-suppressive gas to push fuel gases out. Thus, every time one of the A-4Bs returned with holes in its drop tanks, these were loaded on a truck which brought them to the dry-cleaning shop, which filled them with vapour before they could be repaired by a mechanic.

With regards to operational analysis, the conclusion was unavoidable that the small and nimble A-4Bs, A-4Cs, and A-4Qs of the FAA and the COAN proved the most effective combat aircraft of the war – at least from the

An IA-50 G II taxies behind an A-4C armed with BR bombs. (Vicecomodoro Maiztegui Collection)

Argentine point of view. Obviously, V Brigada Aérea achieved the most. While losing nine pilots and ten aircraft, between 1 May and 13 June 1982 the A-4Bs of its Escuadrón II Aeromóvil caused the loss of one destroyer (HMS *Coventry*), one frigate (HMS *Antelope*), one landing ship logistics (RFA *Sir Galahad*), and a landing craft (*F4*). In other words: the A-4Bs of just this one unit were responsible for more than 60% of the Royal Navy's warship losses during the Malvinas War. Moreover, they moderately damaged the frigate HMS *Argonaut* and the landing ship logistics RFA *Sir Tristram*, while causing slight damage to the destroyer HMS *Glasgow*, and frigates HMS *Brilliant* and HMS *Broadsword*. On the contrary, Escuadrón I Aeromóvil of IV Brigada Aérea, was the least successful of all of the FAA's units: while flying 491.15 hours in combat, it lost nine A-4Cs and eight pilots, while causing only minimal confirmed damage to the British. The scope of this unit's sacrifice for the Argentine claims upon the Islas Malvinas is even more obvious when it's kept in mind that out of 23 pilots deployed in combat during the war, eight were killed, and one captured. How much of this was related to the 'luck factor' is obvious

from the fact that an A-4 pilot of this war, Capitán Carballo, logged a total of 19.55 combat hours during the war, and had his aircraft hit by British air defences no fewer than eight times. Still, he – and members of his flight – were instrumental in the sinking of three Royal Navy warships.

The smallest of the three Argentine A-4 units – 3° Escuadrilla de Caza y Ataque – is known to have flown a total of 39 operational sorties, released 35 Mk.82 bombs (30 of these against naval and 5 against ground targets), fired 662 20mm shells, lost three aircraft (3-A-307, 3-A-312 and 3-A-314) and two pilots.

Overall, the price paid for the FAA's and COAN's achievements was massive: out of 48 A-4s known to have been flown in combat during the war (this total includes 26 A-4Bs, 12 A-4Cs, and 10 A-4Qs), 22 were written off: eight of these to Royal Navy Sea Harriers, five to ship-launched SAMs, four to ground-fire or ground-launched SAMs (including one shot down in a case of fratricide), and five to mishaps or collision with the ground or sea. While up to six pilots ejected successfully, only four were subsequently recovered alive.

9

ARGENTINE SKYHAWKS AFTER THE FALKLANDS/MALVINAS WAR

The A-4Cs of IV Brigada Aérea resumed their flight operations only on 17 June, and were then withdrawn from the combat zone, together with most of the other units of the FAA and COAN between 20 and 25 June 1982. The A-4Bs – meanwhile re-assigned to Escuadrón I Aeromóvil – remained deployed at Río Gallegos. Indeed, such deployments were continued into 1983, and all the combat units were rotated over time. Moreover, the FAA established its X Brigada Aérea equipped with Dassault Mirage IIICs acquired from Israel, and all operational pilots were required to maintain efficiency while training following the lessons learned during the war.[1]

In 1983, the French company Matra obtained the FAA's permission to test-install its R.550 Magic Mk.I short-range infrared-homing air-to-air missiles, Durandal anti-runway bombs and BLG-66 Belouga cluster bomb units (CBUs) on the Skyhawks. The tests for loading, launching and releasing these weapons were carried out without any mishaps by IV Brigada Aérea, with each of the involved A-4Cs being closely monitored by the crew of a Morane-Saulnier Paris trainer, including French personnel.

Despite the good operational status of the unit, by this time IV Brigada Aérea was down to only seven aircraft, while V Brigada Aérea still had 18 (two were lost in post-war accidents in 1982). Therefore, on 31 December 1983, all the A-4Cs were transferred to the later unit. They arrived at Villa Reynolds on the 20th of the same month and

formed the 3rd Squadron of Grupo 5 de Caza.

The following year, the Air Force prepared the first exercise in air combat of dissimilar aircraft types. Designated *Zonda '84*, this took place between 24 and 30 June at Mendoza, and saw the involvement of all the available types of combat aircraft, including Mirage IIICJs, Mirage IIIEAs, Daggers (meanwhile upgraded to the Finger I standard), A-4Bs and A-4Cs, IA.58A Pucaras, F-86F Sabres and even Paris trainers. This exercise proved a big success and was repeated annually until 1990.

Project Escudo

After losing two additional A-4Bs (C-234 and C-237) in 1984, V Brigada Aérea was down to 15 such Skyhawks – and their age was showing, especially in the form of wing cracks, failures of hydraulic and electric systems, deformations in the engine intake, failures of the landing gear, structural vibrations, and abnormal engine noises. However, and despite reaching 140,000 flying hours in 1985, the fleet remained in service. Indeed, in 1986, the old Mk.12 cannons were replaced by 30mm DEFA 553s in the course of Project Escudo (delayed by the Falklands War) undertaken by ARMACUAR. The first aircraft modified this way was F-318, which was also used for all related testing. By 1990, a total of eight A-4s were thus modified.

The rest of the fleet meanwhile took part in such exercises as

The A-4B C-212 with an experimental paint scheme tested after the war, to reduce the visibility of the aircraft.

During and after the war, different paint schemes were tested on the A-4Bs, like this one used by C-212, seen on 13 July 1989.

Another paint scheme tested in the eighties. This aircraft stop flying in 1985.

test-installation of an Omera 110 machine gun was undertaken in June 1989, and subsequently the entire fleet was adapted for the use of such weapons.

The End of the FAA's A-4Bs and A-4Cs

The age of the fleet was meanwhile causing ever more problems: while up to 4,800 hours were flown annually by FAA A-4Bs and A-4Cs in the early 1980s, by 1990, this figure dropped to under 2,800 – and this although one of the Skyhawks became involved in suppressing the rebellion against President Carlos Menem on 3 December of the same year. The FAA was already searching for a replacement and – amongst others – flight-tested Shenyang F-7M interceptors in China (based on the Soviet-made MiG-21), and then Northrop F-5E/F Tiger IIs in Jordan. However, no order was placed due to the lack of money. Later on, the possibility was studied of replacing all of the remaining A-4Bs, A-4Cs, Mirage IIIs and Dagger/Fingers with McDonnell-Douglas F/A-18 Hornets or General Dynamics F-16 Fighting Falcons. However, Washington flatly refused to deliver any Hornets, and in the case of the F-16 replied with, 'not for the moment.' The Skyhawk-fleet thus continued serving and, unsurprisingly, the annual report of the V Brigada Aérea for 1991 concluded that:

…it must be taken into account that this weapons system has almost 34 years of operation (counting its use in the United States), with most of the aircraft near their retirement (at the end of 1991, three aircraft were retired, C-232, 239 and 240) and that the current economic problems that the Air Force is experiencing have affected the ability to process repairable items in the Material Areas and also in 5th Technical Group, the lack of raw material seriously penalises the possibility of doing a good preventive maintenance forcing [us] to make only restorative maintenance, that is, repair as new developments occur, with the risks that this philosophy entails, since sometimes this type of repairs are more expensive for the material and personnel.

Still, the A-4Bs and A-4Cs continued serving. Indeed, between

Primavera in September, and *Gaucón* in October. However, on 14 November 1986, C-240 broke the in-flight refuelling hose of one of the KC-130Hs and suffered from the entry of fuel into the intakes: the pilot managed a successful emergency landing, but subsequently all the further IFR-operations were suspended.

In March 1988, surviving A-4Bs and A-4Cs took part in the suitably dubbed Exercise *Halcón*, staged from the airfield of Mar del Plata. Two squadrons were also re-deployed to Comodoro Rivadavia for Exercise *Orion*, in September of the same year. While Project *Escudo* was meanwhile continued at Rio IV – despite a mishap in which the A-4B used as the prototype was lost while flown by TT Claudio Castro (who ejected safely) – another improvement was added in the form of replacing the old MF-1 gun-sight with the Libescope. Moreover, a

19 and 24 March 1991, an Esquadron Aeromóvil was re-deployed to IX Brigada Aérea Comodoro Rivadavia, and in September their crews ran live firing exercises at the range in Antuna, before returning to Comodoro Rivadavia for a tactical shooting contest in October. Moreover, regular fragmentary orders for re-deployments to Tandil were completed at the request of the Air Operations command. Unsurprisingly considering such an intensity of operations, the fleet was temporarily grounded in August and one A-4C – C-312 – was lost in an accident on 1 October (PT Mario Rovella ejected safely), thus reducing the number of available aircraft to 15.

With the remaining A-4Bs and A-4Cs completing their life cycle, the decision was taken to replace them by A-4Ms upgraded to the standard designated the A-4AR. The original plan was to acquire 54 such aircraft, but this was reduced to 32 single-seaters and four two-seaters, and an order placed in 1993. The delivery was much delayed and the first A-4AR Fighting Hawk reached Argentina only on 19 December 1997 – by when only eight A-4Bs were still in operational condition. As the A-4ARs entered service, remaining A-4Bs and A-4Cs were grouped into the 3rd Squadron of Groupo 5 de Caza and then their operations slowed down. The A-4Bs were officially retired on 15 March 1999 – the 50th anniversary of the FAA's brigades – thus closing this chapter in the history of the Argentine Air Force.

The End of Naval Skyhawks

The severely depleted 3º Escuadrilla Aeronaval de Caza y Ataque returned to Base Aeronaval Comandante Espora in June 1982. It embarked six aircraft (four of these with new wings) on ARA *25 de Mayo* on 15 and 16 October, and then on 25-28 October 1982 again, for the first time together with new Super Etendards, and then in joint exercises with the Brazilian navy. By November 1982, the fleet was down to four operational aircraft, because 3-A-302 was in such a poor condition that it could not be operated from an aircraft carrier again, and then TC Loubet Jambert was killed in the crash of 3-A-306.[2]

A-4C C-314 refuelling from a Hercules. Since its transference to V Brigada Aérea this aircraft carried the badges of both units.

An Argentine Air Force A-4B and a Navy Super Etendard refuelling from a KC-130H.

Line of 17 A-4B and at least one A-4C (at the end) in 1992, when Grupo 5 de Caza could achieve 30 operational Skyhawks of both models.

An installation of DEFA 553 guns, Librascope sights, radio altimeter, the Hoffman AN/RNA-91 TACAN and VLF Omega Series II was evaluated, but never applied. Instead, the small fleet continued serving through routine exercises in 1983 and 1984, by when only three aircraft were left in operational condition, but all were equipped with chaff and flare launchers and a digital intervalometer. That said, a reinforcement was in sight: during the Falklands War, in May 1982, Argentina placed an order for 12 A-4Es in Israel, modified through the addition of the Elbit Low Cost Weapons Delivery and Navigation System (including an inertial navigation system), and a head-up display. Works began in late 1984, and the aircraft were expected to arrive a

An A-4B and an A-4C flying next to a KC-130H Hercules tanker.

An A-4C flying with a Matra R-550 Magic test missile, during the homologation of the missiles on the planes, to replace the Shafrir 2.

A-4C C-314 and A-4B C-225 taking off from V Brigada Aérea during a training flight on September 1998. (Photo by Santiago Rivas)

A-4C serial C-322 taking off from V Brigada Aérea in 1998. (Photo by Santiago Rivas)

year later.[3] However, such an export had to be authorised by Washington: although Buenos Aires had already paid for 80% of the aircraft and their upgrade, the US government refused to authorise this deal. Thus, instead of selling Skyhawks to Argentina, the Israelis overhauled and re-engined the remaining S-2E Trackers and provided three additional Sergeant Fletcher 31-300 IFR-pods.

3° Escuadrilla thus continued flying its old A-4Qs. One of these, 3-A-305, lost power on 22 May 1986, forcing the pilot, TF José Plá, to eject safely. In July of the same year, the unit reembarked its last four aircraft – 3-A-301, 3-A-302, 3-A-304, and 3-A-309 – on board ARA *25 de Mayo* for the last time, and the first of these received the honour of making the final catapult launch from the carrier. The 3-A-304 was subsequently withdrawn from service, and 3° Escuadrilla was integrated into 2° Escuadrilla, where it operated its last two Skyhawks alongside the Super Etendards. For a while at least, a continuation of their service was contemplated in the form of using them for IFR-operations, reconnaissance, electronic warfare, or training, but all such designs had to be abandoned for the lack of funding. The last two A-4Qs were de-activated on 25 February 1988 in the course of a formal ceremony at Base Aeronaval Comandante Espora: Teniente de Navio Medici had the honour of making the final flight with 3-A-302 (which for this purpose had received a wing from 3-A-308) to Aeroparque Jorge Newbery in Buenos Aires. This aircraft is presently on display at the Naval Aviation Museum of Comandante Espora.

A-4Q 3-A-308 was the only Skyhawk of 3° Escuadrilla to survive the war without being camouflaged. 3-A-306 carried those colours for a short time before being lost in an accident on 16 December 1982.

By 1983 the A-4Qs had reverted to their original paint scheme. This picture shows one of the few times they embarked together with the Super Etendards.

3-A-302 seen in the mid-1980s at Base Aeronaval Comandante Espora.

Two of the A-4Es intended for the Argentine Navy. The one behind wears the Argentine colours but without the flag and markings.

By 1984 the A-4Qs had received a new paint scheme, with blue grey on the upper part and the lower part and markings in light grey. This scheme was also adopted by the Trackers, Sea Kings, EMB-326 Xavantes and other aircraft of COAN.

When the Brazilian Navy decided to buy the A-4KUs, their carrier NAeL *Minas Gerais* went to Base Naval Puerto Belgrano, where A-4Q 3-A-302, by then at the Naval Aviation Museum, was embarked to test the operation of the Skyhawk on the deck and hangar of the aircraft carrier. (Photo Martín García)

APPENDIX
INDIVIDUAL ARGENTINE SKYHAWKS

Table 8: A-4Cs of IV Brigada Aére, Fuerza Aérea Argentina

Serial	C/n or Bu.No.	Enlisted	Notes
C-301	147714	1976	Shot down 30 May 1982 by HMS *Exeter*. Pilot TT Vázquez killed.
C-302	148438	1976	Retired in 1997. At Museo Nacional de Malvinas, at Oliva, Córdoba.
C-303	149526	1976	Crashed on Jason Islands on 9 May 1982. Lt Farías killed.
C-304	149618	1976	Shot down by HMS *Coventry* on 25 May 1982. Pilot Captain García ejected but was never recovered.
C-305	148562	1976	Shot down on 24 May 1982, Lt Bono killed.
C-309	147747	1976	Shot down on 21 May 1982 by Sea Harrier XZ492 flown by TT Cdr. Neil Thomas. TT López killed.
C-310	148450	1976	Shot down by HMS *Exeter* on 30 May 1982. PT Castillo killed.
C-312	147765	1976	Survived the war, crashed on 3 October 1991, pilot PT Mario Rovella ejected.
C-313	150595	1976	Crashed on Jason Islands on 9 May 1982, TT Casco killed.
C-314	149564	1976	Retired on 29 March 1999, preserved at IV Brigada Aérea.
C-318	148556	1976	Survived the war and crashed at V Brigada Aérea on 3 October 1988, TT Claudio Castro ejected.
C-319	148553	1976	Shot down by a SAM on 25 May 1982, TT Ricardo Lucero ejected.
C-321	147741	1976	Survived the war and crashed on 10 March 1995 at San Luis, PT Mario Bordagaray killed.
C-322	149541	1976	Retired on 29 March 1999 and preserved at the Museo Nacional de Aeronáutica at Morón, made the last flight of the model.
C-324	148559	1976	Survived the war and lost in an accident at V Brigada Aérea on 10 December 1997, Captain Hugo Ludueña ejected.
C-325	149585	1976	Shot down by Lt Cdr. Mike Blisset in Sea Harrier XZ496 on 21 May. Pilot PT Manzotti killed.

Table 9: A-4Bs of the V Brigada Aére, Fuerza Aérea Argentina

Serial	C/n or Bu. No.	Enlisted	Notes
C-204	142126	31-10-66	Participated in the attack against HMS *Ardent* on 21 May 1982 and shot down on its sixth mission by Sea Harrier XZ499 commanded by Lt David Smith at Pleasant Bay on 8 June. Sank the landing craft *F4*. PT Danilo Bolzán killed.
C-206	142742	31-10-66	Hit the water on its third mission while trying to evade a Sea Wolf missile from HMS *Brilliant* on 12 May 1982. TT Nivoli killed.
C-207	142688	31-10-66	Flew seven attack missions and took part on the attack against HMS *Coventry* but the bombs didn't leave the aircraft. Retired on 29 March 1999 and preserved at the Museo Nacional de Aeronáutica at Morón.
C-208	142139	18-3-67	Shot down on 12 May 1982 by a Sea Wolf from HMS *Brilliant*. Lt Jorge R. Ibarlucea killed.
C-209	142684	31-10-66	Survived the war, destroyed on 23 June 1994 in an accident at Salar del Tolillar. Pilot unharmed.
C-212	142773	31-10-66	Flew twelve missions during the war, attacked the merchant ship Formosa by mistake and sank HMS *Coventry*. Survived the war, damaged in an accident at Santa Cruz on 10 December 1985. Now a monument at Río IV workshops with serial C-302.
C-214	142109	31-10-66	Flew 8 missions and attacked HMS *Broadsword* and RFA *Sir Tristram*. Retired on 31 March 1999. Preserved at V Brigada Aérea.
C-215	142102	31-10-66	Attacked the merchant ship *Formosa* by mistake, damaged HMS *Argonaut* and RFA *Sir Lancelot*. Shot down on 27 May 1982 by HMS *Intrepid* on its fifth mission, PT Mariano Velasco ejected.
C-221	142108	18-3-67	Flew six missions, stopped flying in 1996 and retired on 29 March 1999.
C-222	142752	18-3-67	Called El Tordillo because it was painted grey. Flew four missions, sank RFA *Sir Galahad*. Retired on 29 March 1999, preserved at the Río IV workshop museum.
C-224	142132	18-3-67	Took part on the attack against HMS *Argonaut*, retired in 1995. Monument at Ezeiza Petty Officers School.

C-225	142803	18-3-67	Flew six missions and attacked the merchant ship *Formosa* by mistake and damaged HMS *Broadsword*. Retired on 15 March 1999 and used at the Escuela de Suboficiales de Fuerza Aérea at Córdoba for ground training.
C-226	142090	6-69	Damaged RFA *Sir Galahad* on 21 May 1982 and was shot down by Sea Harrier ZA177 flown by Flt Lt David Morgan on 8 June after sinking landing craft *F4* in Pleasant Bay. Lt Arrarás killed.
C-227	142104	6-69	Survived the war and was lost in an accident on 3 August 1987 during an attack exercise, pilot TT Olivieri killed.
C-228	142728	6-69	Shot down on its fourth mission by Sea Harrier ZA177 flown by Flt Lt David Morgan on 8 June 1982 after sinking landing craft *F4* in Pleasant Bay. Pilot Alférez Vázquez killed.
C-230	142736	6-69	Flew five combat missions and damaged RFA *Sir Tristram*. Lost in an accident on 21 September 1982 at Las Isletas, close to V Brigada Aérea. Pilot Alférez Luoni killed.
C-231	142748	6-69	Retired in 1992 and is now a monument at the entrance of V Brigada Aérea.
C-232	142749	6-69	Retired on September 1991.
C-233	142757	6-69	Retired in 1992 and is a monument at IV Brigada Aérea painted as A-4C with serial C-301.
C-234	142760	6-69	Survived the war and was lost in an accident close to base on 31 October 1984, pilot ejected.
C-235	142765	6-69	Survived the war and was lost in an accident near 9 de Julio, Buenos Aires, on 13 July 1983, pilot ejected.
C-236	142784	6-69	Survived the war and was lost in an accident at Loma del Toro, Neuquen, on 4 October 1988, pilot ejected.
C-237	142788	4-70	Survived the war and was lost in an accident at Vicuña Mackenna, Córdoba, on 19 November 1984, pilot ejected.
C-239	142838	4-70	Flew seven combat missions and damaged HMS *Brilliant*, retired in 1991 and donated to the company IMPSA for its help to the Air Force.
C-240	142855	4-70	Flew six combat missions, attacked the merchant ship ELMA *Formosa* by mistake, and HMS *Argonaut* and HMS *Antelope*. Retired in 1991 and preserved on Buenos Aires domestic airport military tarmac.
C-242	142862	4-70	Destroyed on its third mission on 23 May 1982 when it hit HMS *Antelope*'s main mast. One of its bombs hit the ship, which was sunk. TT Luciano Guadagnini killed.
C-244	142883	4-70	Shot down by a Sea Dart from HMS *Coventry* on 25 May 1982 on its fourth mission, pilot Captain Del Valle Palaver killed.
C-246	142901	4-70	Shot down on 12 May 1982 by a Sea Wolf from HMS *Brilliant*, PT Bustos killed.
C-248	142910	4-70	Shot down by own artillery fire over BAM Cóndor on 12 May 1982 after damaging HMS *Glasgow*. PT Fausto Gavazzi killed.
C-250	142914	4-70	Survived the war and lost in an accident at San Rafael, Mendoza, on 12 November 1982, pilot ejected.

Table 10: A-4Qs of 3° Escuadrilla

Serial	Callsign	Bureau Number	Enlisted	Notes
0654	3-A-301	144872	1972	Former 3-A-201. Retired in 1987, preserved at the Escuela de Educación Técnica N8 Jorge Newbery for ground training.
0655	3-A-302	144882	1972	Former 3-A-202 Retired in 1988 and preserved at the Museo de la Aviación Naval. At Comandante Espora.
0657	3-A-304	144915	1972	Former 3-A-204. Retired in 1987 and is a monument at the Argentine Navy Headquarters.
0658	3-A-305	144929	1972	Former 3-A-205. Lost in an accident over BACE on 22 May 1986.
0659	3-A-306	144963	1972	Former 3-A-206. Lost in an accident at BACE on 16 December 1982.
0660	3-A-307	144983	1972	Former 3-A-207. Shot down by Lt Morrell in Sea Harrier XZ457 on 21 May 1982. CC Philippi ejected.
0661	3-A-308	144988	1972	Former 3-A-208. Retired in 1984 and preserved as a monument at Aeroclub Batan (Mar del Plata) with callsign 3-A-214.
0662	3-A-309	144989	1972	Former 3-A-209. Retired in 1987. Sold to a private owner in the USA on 2 September 1998.
0665	3-A-312	145010	1972	Former 3-A-212. TN Arca ejected safely after being hit by Lt Morrell in Sea Harrier XZ457 on 21 May 1982. Airplane shot down by own artillery because it endangered the pilot on his descent to the sea.
0667	3-A-314	145050	1972	Former 3-A-214. Shot down on 21 May 1982 by Flt Lt Leeming in Sea Harrier XZ500. TF Márquez killed.

BIBLIOGRAPHY

Amores, E., *Fuerza Aérea Argentina, Guía de aeronaves militares, 1912-2006* (Buenos Aires: Dirección de Estudios Históricos de la FAA, 2007).

Brown, D., *The Royal Navy and the Falklands War: The Epic, True Story* (London: Arrow Books Ltd., 1989).

Burden, R. and others, *Falklands: The Air War* (London: British Aviation Research Group, 1986).

Cal, C., Sequeira, S. y Calatayud, C., *Aviación Naval Argentina* (Buenos Aires: SS&CC Ediciones, 1984).

Carballo, P. M., *Dios y los Halcones* (Buenos Aires: Editorial Abril, 1983).

Carballo, P. M. *Halcones sobre Malvinas* (Buenos Aires: Ediciones del Cruzamante, 1984).

Eddy, P., Linklater, M. & Gillman P., *Una cara de la moneda* (Montevideo: Editorial Hyspamérica, 1988).

Elward, B., *McDonnell Douglas A-4 Skyhawk* (Ramsbury: Crowood Aviation Series, 2000).

Historia de la Fuerza Aérea Argentina, Tomo VI, La Guerra de Malvinas Volume 1 y 2 (Buenos Aires: Dirección de Estudios Históricos de la FAA, 2000).

Historia de la Aviación Naval Argentina, Tomo III, La Guerra de Malvinas (Buenos Aires: Instituto de Publicaciones Navales, 1991).

Hobson, C. & Noble, A., *Falklands Air War* (Hinckley: Ian Allan Publishing, 2002).

Huertas, S. M., 'A-4 Skyhawk in the Falklands', *Wings of Fame*, Volume 12, 1998.

Huertas, S. M., *La Guerre des Malouines*, (Outreau: Editions Lela Presse, 2000).

Huertas, S. M., & Romero, Major B. J, *Falklands: Witness of Battles* (Valencia: Editorial Federico Domenech, 1985).

Kilduff, P., *Douglas A-4 Skyhawk* (London: Osprey Air Combat, 1983).

Matassi, P., *La Batalla Aérea por nuestras islas Malvinas* (Buenos Aires: Editorial Halcón Cielo, 1990).

McKay, F., & Cooksey, J., *Pebble Island: Operation Prelim* (Barnsley: Pen & Sword Ltd., 2007).

McManners, H., *Forgotten Voices of the Falklands* (London: Ebury Publishing, 2008).

Morgan, D. *Hostile Skies, The Battle for the Falklands* (London: Phoenix, 2007).

Moro, R. O., *La Guerra Inaudita* (Buenos Aires: Editorial Pleamar, 1985).

Nuñez Padin, J., *A-4P Skyhawk; Serie Fuerza Aérea Nº 26* (Bahia Blanca: Fuerzas Aeronavales, 2016).

Nuñez Padin, J, *A-4C Skyhawk; Serie Fuerza Aérea Nº 21* (Bahia Blanca: Fuerzas Aeronavales, 2011).

Nuñez Padin, J., *McDonnell Douglas A-4Q & A-4E Skyhawk* (Neuquén, Serie Aeronaval Nº31, 2013).

Price, A. & Ethell, J., *Air War South Atlantic* (London: Sidgwick & Jackson, 1983).

Ramsey, G., *The Falklands War: then and now* (London: Battle of Britain International Ltd, 2009).

Rivas, S., *Wings of the Malvinas, the Argentine air war over the Falklands* (Manchester: Crécy Publishing, 2012).

Rivas, S. & Cicalesi, J. C., *Malvinas 1982* (São Paulo: C&R Editorial, 2007).

Rivas, S. & Cicalesi, J. C., *La Guerre des Malouines* (Paris: Editions TMA, 2008).

Smith, G., *Battles of the Falklands War* (Shepperton: Ian Allan Publishing, 1989).

Thomason, T., *Scooter! The Douglas A-4 Skyhawk Story* (Manchester: Crécy Publishing Ltd., 2011).

Villarino, E., *Exocet* (Buenos Aires: Editorial Abril, 1983).

Ward, N., *Sea Harrier over the Falklands: A Maverick at War* (London: BCA, 1992).

Winchester, J., *Douglas A-4 Skyhawk, Attack & Close-support Fighter Bomber* (Barnsley: Pen & Sword, 2005).

Woodward, J. F., *Los cien días* (Buenos Aires: Editorial Sudamericana, 1992).

Interviews
Brigadier Alejandro Amoros
Brigadier Mario Roca
Brigadier Guillermo Dellepiane
Comodoro Pablo M. Carballo
Comodoro Gerardo Isaac
Comodoro Ernesto Ureta
Comodoro Mariano Velasco
Comodoro Horacio Mir González
Comodoro Héctor Sánchez
Mayor Luis Cervera
Capitán Marcelo Moroni
Contraalmirante Benito Rótolo
Contraalmirante José César Arca
Capitán de Navío Roberto Sylvester
Capitán de Corbeta (en 1982) Rodolfo Castro Fox
Lt Cdr. Nigel Ward (801 Squadron)
David Smith (800 Squadron)
Able Seaman (M) Neil Wilkinson (HMS Intrepid)
Martin Dunkin (HMS Intrepid)
Flt Lt David Morgan (800 Squadron)
Hugh McManners
Salvador Mafé Huertas
Juan Carlos Cicalesi
Hernán Casciani
Jorge Nuñez Padín
Ricky Strange

Imperial War Museum Sound Archive
16817 Radio Supervisor Stewart Anthony MacFarlane, HMS *Coventry*
14154 TT Cdr. Graham J. Edmonds, Operations Officer and Squadron Warfare Office, HMS *Broadsword*
11307 TT Cdr. Raymond Adams, HMS *Coventry*

Institutions
Dirección de Estudios Históricos de la Fuerza Aérea Argentina.
Memoirs of the Argentine Air Force and the Argentine Navy.
Instituto Aeronaval.
Biblioteca Nacional de Aeronáutica

Magazines
Salvador Mafé Huertas, 'Tábanos em combate', *Fuerza Aérea, No1*

Salvador Mafé Huertas, 'Tábanos em combate II', *Fuerza Aérea Clásica No.1*

Internet

Royal Air Force; www.raf.mod.uk

NOTES

Introduction

1 Note that both British and Argentine names for locations in and around the Falkland Islands are used throughout this text. The use of one or other name at any given point within the text should not be construed as implying the paramountcy of one name above the other.

2 Note that all references to the FAA refer to the Fuerza Aérea Argentina and not to the Royal Navy's Fleet Air Arm.

3 The reader should bear in mind that sections of this book are based on the testimony of those involved and that human recollection is often far from perfect. These recollections may differ to varying degrees from those of other participants in the events described and from versions of events in other histories of the war. These testimonies are presented in good faith as they convey the impressions and recollections of the Argentine A-4 pilots engaged in the war.

Chapter 1

1 The V Brigada Aérea used British-made Avro Lancaster and Avro Lincoln bombers before converting to A-4 Skyhawks.

2 These first aircraft were transferred to Argentina by the following pilots: C-201, VC Ruiz; C-202, Capitán Rodriguez Morell; C-204, Capitán Juan Manuel Baigorria; C-205, Primer Teniente (PT) Joaquín Pedro Solabarrietta; C-206, VC Luis Fernando Masserini; C-207, Capitán Hector Oscar Panzardi; C-209, Capitán Juan Carlos Gabarret; C-211, PT Andrés Arnold Antonietti; C-212, Major Héctor René Roy; C-215, Capitán Juan Francisco Laskowski; C-214, Major Juan Raúl Boelher; and C-213, Capitán Luis Héctor Destri.

3 IX Brigada Aérea was created at that base on 9 December 1975. Until then it was BAM Comodoro Rivadavia.

Chapter 2

1 Despite the acquisition of A-4Cs, the F-86Fs remained in service until 1986.

2 'The Israel Aircraft Industries Dagger' was actually the Dassault-manufactured Mirage 5J, produced in France, but – with US support – clandestinely delivered to Israel in the form of knock-down kits in 1970 -1971, and assembled with the help of engineers from the Rockwell Corporation.

Chapter 3

1 Contrary to what is often reported in the English-language media, 25 de Mayo is the date celebrated in Argentina as the *Día de la Revolución de Mayo*, or 'May Revolution Day', not the nation's 'Independence Day'. Correspondingly, writing the designation of this aircraft carrier in letters – as is frequently done in English-language publications – is incorrect.

2 In addition to its own capacity of 900-litres, the Sergeant Fletcher could, once it had transferred its own fuel, automatically draws fuel from the wing-tanks and transfer this as well. This was possible because the A-4Q consumed its fuel in the following order: drop tanks first, then the wing tank and then the fuselage tank.

3 In Argentina it is also known by the Navy as EA33 as it was the 3º Eacuadrilla Aeronaval de Caza y Ataque of the Escuadra Aeronaval No.3. The designation is frequently shortened to 3º Escuadrilla in diverse English-language publications. While, 'theoretically correct', such a designation was never used by the ARA.

4 The A-4 in question was a veteran of US operations over the Bay of Pigs, in Cuba, in 1961: at that time this A-4 was flown from the aircraft carrier USS *Essex* (CV-9).

Chapter 4

1 The rank of a Brigadier-General in the FAA is equal to that of a Lieutenant-General.

2 BRP stood for *Bomba Retardad por Paracaídstas*, or parachute retarded bomb.

Chapter 5

1 That the Argentineans were right in their conclusions is shown by such British recollections as those by Flight Lieutenant David Morgan, an RAF pilot that flew Sea Harriers with NAS 800 from HMS *Hermes* during the Falklands War, who explained to the author during an interview: 'I flew some DACT (Dissimilar Air Combat Training) against the US Navy aggressor squadron A-4s at NAS Oceana in 1986. It was very similar to the Hunter; good in a turning fight but nowhere near the Sea Harrier in regards of climbing capability.'

2 For precise details about the movement of TF.79.1 in these and during the following days, see the sister-publication *A Carrier at Risk*, by Mariano Sciaroni (details in the bibliography).

3 'Type 64' and '42-22 combo' came from the designations of the two ship classes: destroyers like HMS *Sheffield*, HMS *Coventry*, HMS *Glasgow*, and HMS *Exeter* belonged to the Type 42 class, while frigates like HMS *Broadsword*, HMS *Battleaxe* and HMS *Brilliant* belonged to the Type 22 class.

4 All three pilots killed in action were posthumously promoted in rank.

Chapter 6

1 Underwood, p. 63.

2 Ibid.

3 For one of the typical British accounts, see Brown, *The Royal Navy and the Falklands War*, p. 317. The first semi-official account of the FAA's involvement in this conflict was published in *Aerospacio* magazine, November/December 1983. The same source listed the number of sorties launched by the FAA as 33 on 21 May, 46 on 23 May, and 16 on 25 May.

4 McKay et al p.99. Aware of the Argentines now knowing his position, the skipper of HMS *Coventry*, Captain David Hart Dyke requested permission to re-deploy to a new position, further north and between the mainland and the islands. However, this was denied by Admiral Woodward, who though the idea would expose the two valuable ships to Exocet attack.

5 London later reported that 170 of HMS *Coventry's* crew were rescued by HMS *Broadsword*, and the official memorial plaque for those who died in the loss of the destroyer at Holy Trinity Church in Coventry cites 19 names. None of the officers or other ranks of the Royal Navy involved in this catastrophe has ever received any awards for bravery.

Chapter 7

1 Spanish for 'Return with Honour'and the motto of the Grupo 4 de Cazabombardeo, IV Brigada Aérea.

2 Indeed, the aircraft in question were five Pucaras of Gaucho Flight, arriving from the mainland.

3 Grupo 2 Vigilancia y Control Aereo, *Daily Report to the CdoFAS*, 30 May 1982 (FAA Historical Branch).

4 Editorial note: it is suggested in the strongest possible terms that the interested reader investigate a broad range of source material regarding this matter as in many respects this version of events has taken on the characteristics of a conspiracy theory. In the interests of balance, David Brown's *The Royal Navy and the Falkland's War* (London: Arrow Book Limited, 1987), for example, says that "The Exocet was detected by both the *Exeter*, whose third Sea Dart had been fired at it, and the *Avenger*, which claimed to have destroyed it with her opening 4.5in rounds, but it was not seen by either ship and may have been decoyed to the west of its intended track by the frigate's chaff" and states that *Invincible* flew more Sea Harrier sorties in the days immediately after the attack than in the days immediately preceding it. p. 256. Sandy Woodward's account in

One Hundred Days (London: Harper*press*, 2012) describes the Exocet as passing harmlessly between *Exeter* and *Avenger* and refers to the Argentine accounts of this matter as "fantasies." pp. 430-431. It remains that nothing that could be described as independently verifiable evidence has been produced to support the Argentine pilots' version of events and, as is evidenced in several instances elsewhere in this book, pilots under the enormous stress of combat conditions often misidentified the vessels that they had attacked.

Chapter 8

1   Morgan, p. 265.

2   Ibid, p. 267.

Chapter 9

1   Notably, while originally designated Mirage IIICJ in the Israeli service, these aircraft were designated only Mirage IIIC in the FAA's service.

2   The A-4Q 3-A-306 thus became the only Argentinean naval aircraft to take the lives of two of its pilots.

3   Indeed, the Israeli A-4Es destined for Argentina had already received serials 3-A-301 to 3-A-312 and six were already painted in dark grey, pending their delivery: the upgrade through the addition of the Low Cost Weapons Delivery and Navigation System was to take place in Argentina.

ABOUT THE AUTHOR

Santiago Rivas was born in Buenos Aires, Argentina, in 1977. After graduating in journalism, since 1997 he began to work in aviation and defence journalism, travelling all across Latin America to conduct his research for articles and books. In 2007 he published his first book, about the Falklands/Malvinas War in Brazil, and since then has penned 18 additional volumes in Argentina, Brazil, France, Germany, Austria and the United Kingdom. He had also published articles in more than 50 magazines in 20 countries and currently works for more than twenty such publications. Rivas has three children and lives in Buenos Aires.